WAR IN EUROPE

Illustrated by
Belinda Swanson and Nigel Martindale

WAR IN EUROPE

Fiona Reynoldson

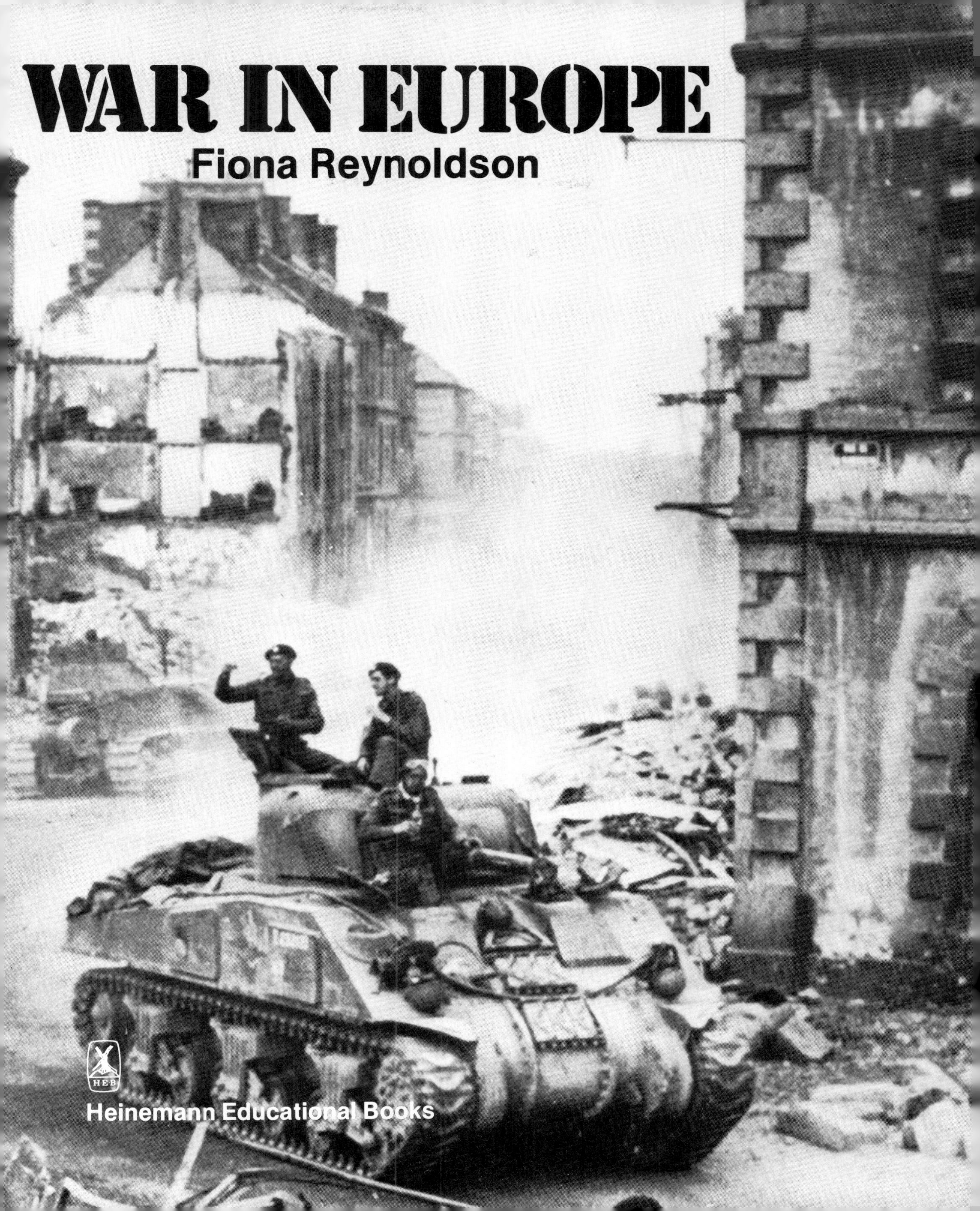

HEB

Heinemann Educational Books

TITLE PAGE ILLUSTRATION: *Sherman tanks moving through northern France two months after D-Day.*

Heinemann Educational Books Ltd
22 Bedford Square, London WC1B 3HH
LONDON EDINBURGH MELBOURNE
AUCKLAND HONG KONG SINGAPORE
KUALA LUMPUR NEW DELHI IBADAN
NAIROBI JOHANNESBURG EXETER (NH)
KINGSTON PORT OF SPAIN

First published 1980

British Library Cataloguing in Publication Data

Reynoldson, Fiona
War in Europe. – (The Second World War; 2).
1. World War, 1939–45 – Campaigns – Western
I. Title II. Series
940.54′21 D756
ISBN 0-435-31881-0

Filmset and printed in Great Britain by BAS Printers Limited, Over Wallop, Hampshire

CONTENTS

ACKNOWLEDGEMENTS

The author and publishers wish to thank the following for permission to reproduce photographs and drawings on the pages indicated:
B.B.C. Hulton Picture Library: pp. 1, 2, 2–3, 6, 23, 24 and 58 (lower).
Camera Press: pp. 12 (lower), 15 and 58 (top).
Illustrated London News: pp. 11 and 46.
Imperial War Museum: pp. 5, 7, 9, 10 (lower), 12 (top), 13, 26 (top), 30–31, 35, 36, 39, 40, 41, 47, 49, 50, 51, 61 (top), 63, 64 and 68.
Keystone: p. 10 (top).
Overlord Embroidery Trustees: pp. 60 and 61 (lower).
Popperfoto: title page, p. 20 (top).

1 THE RISE OF HITLER

Hitler at a Nazi rally in Dortmund in 1933.

The Young Hitler

Adolf Hitler became the German leader. He was born in 1889. His father was a customs officer. Hitler did not like his father. His father wanted him to work hard and get a good job. Hitler was lazy at school. He was often in trouble because he did not do his work. He wanted to be an artist. He was quite good at art. He was not good enough to go to a special art school. He drew some pictures for postcards. He did not earn enough money to live well. He became a tramp. He did not know what to do with his life.

Hitler as a soldier

Then in 1914 the First World War started. Hitler became a soldier. He loved being a soldier. He was brave and won a medal called the Iron Cross. Near the end of the war he was gassed. He was very ill and nearly became blind. He recovered when the war was nearly over. He was horrified. His beloved Germany had lost the war. It was 1918.

Britain, France and America won the First World War. The Germans were very bitter because they lost it. They could not believe that they had lost fairly. They thought that they had been betrayed. They wondered if their government had been bribed with money to give up the war.

Hitler addressing the Nazi Party Congress at Nuremberg, 1938.

Hitler and Himmler inspecting the S.S. guard.

The Nazi Party

Germany had to pay for damage that she had done in the war. This made her poor. Hitler felt very bitter too. He wanted to lead his country. He wanted Germany to be a great country again. Hitler joined together with some others. They formed a group called the Nazi Party. They were working to make Germany great and rich again. Gradually the Nazi Party became bigger. More and more German people joined it. They went to listen to Hitler speaking. He spoke wonderfully. People stood and listened to him for two hours without moving. They believed everything he said. He said he would make Germany great. He would find them all jobs. He would make them rich. They followed Hitler because they wanted to be great and rich.

Hitler as a German leader

Hitler became the leader of Germany in 1933. Some Germans did not like him or the Nazi Party. They said the Nazis were brutal. They also said that Hitler and the Nazis had stopped

people being able to vote for the government they wanted. Hitler did not like these things being said. He put these people in prison.

Hitler hated Jewish people. There were many Jews in Germany then. They did not do any harm. They did not speak against Hitler but Hitler put them in prison. These Jews were cruelly treated in prison. Many suffered horribly. Many died.

Hitler had a private army. This was called the *Schutz Staffeln*. It was know as the S.S. for short. He also made a secret police force called the Gestapo. The S.S. and the Gestapo made sure that no one disobeyed Hitler.

Children were brought up to love Hitler. They were told they must tell their teachers if anyone spoke against Hitler. They were to tell their teachers if their parents spoke against Hitler. Then their parents were put in prison.

Germany wanted more land

Germany became stronger. Her army was made bigger. Her air force was made bigger. Her navy was made bigger. Hitler wanted more land. He wanted to make a great German Empire. It would be called the Third Reich.

By 1938, he was ready to take more land. Look at the map. He turned on Austria, marked (1) on the map. The Austrians gave up without a fight. Hitler turned on Czechoslovakia (2). He took part of Czechoslovokia in 1938. The next year he took the rest of Czechoslovakia (3). In September 1939 he took Poland (4).

Britain and France were worried. Where would Hitler go next? Perhaps he might turn on France and then on Britain. Neither Britain nor France wanted to be conquered by Germany. They declared war on Germany in September 1939.

Countries taken by Hitler.

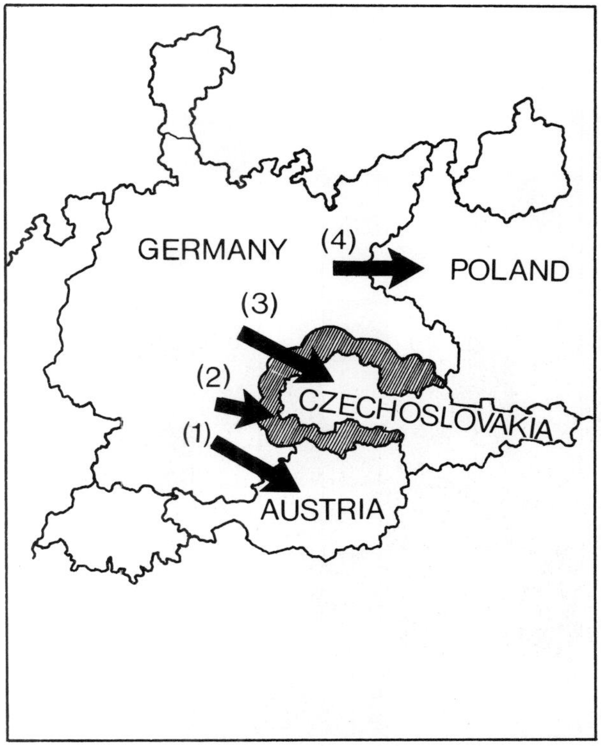

Things to Do

1 Fill in the gaps. (*Numbers in brackets refer to text line numbers.*)
The German leader was called ––––– ––––––– (1). He became a soldier in the ––––– ––––– War (16). Germany lost that war. Hitler wanted to make –––––––– (37) a great country again. He formed a group called the ––––– (40) Party. Hitler became very powerful. He began to take land from other countries. In September 1939 he took ––––––– (99). This made France and –––––––– (106) declare war on Germany.

2 Why did people follow Hitler?

3 Look at the map on page 3. Make a list of the countries which Hitler took.

4. What was the job of the S.S. and the Gestapo?

5 Do the crossword.

Numbers in brackets after some clues refer to text line numbers

ACROSS

1 '––––– Hitler became the German leader.' (1)
5 'They followed Hitler because they wanted to be great and ––––.' (53)
7 '––––––– hated Jewish people.' (64)
8 Short for *Schutz Staffeln.*
9 Opposite of don't.
10 Opposite of yes.
11 'Some Germans did not like him or the –––– Party.' (56)
12 '–––––––– had to pay for damage that she had done in the war.' (34)
14 'He wanted Germany –– be a great country again.' (37)
15 'He also made a secret police force called the ––––––––.' (73)
18 'He drew some pictures ––– postcards.' (11)

DOWN

2 'He was ––––– in trouble because he did not do his work.' (6)
3 Short for Frederick.
4 'The Germans were very bitter because they –––– it.' (27)
6 'He was brave and won a medal called the –––– –––––.' (18)
7 'People stood and listened to him for two ––––– without moving.' (47)
13 A word meaning a short sleep.
14 For how many hours would people stand and listen to Hitler?
16 'He wanted to be –– artist.' (8)
17 'The next year he took the rest –– Czecholslovakia.' (98)

2 THE BEGINNING OF THE WAR

Poland

Poland was a long way from Britain. How could Britain help Poland? The answer was very little. Britain had a very small army. Germany had a huge one. Britain's army was short of up-to-date weapons. Germany had plenty of tanks, guns and lorries.

Britain did have a very good navy. That was not much use in helping Poland.

Britain's air force was small. Germany's was very large.

So, at first, Britain did nothing. Britain and France waited to see what would happen. Poland fought hard but they were badly defeated by Germany. The Germans bombed their airfields. They bombed their cities. They used dive-bombers which were called Stukas. They made a screaming noise. This was terrifying. Many Poles died. On 24 September 1939, 1,150 German aeroplanes bombed Warsaw. Warsaw is the biggest city in Poland. The bombing was so bad that there was no time to bury anyone. People made wooden crosses. They put them on the rubble to show where their families had died.

Then the Germans swept in with their tanks and took over. Poland was no longer a country. Germany divided it with Russia.

A Stuka (Junkers Ju 87).

Germany blew up British ships

What would Germany do next? She worked hard to blow up Britain's ships. Britain had many ships. She needed them. The Germans knew this. They invented a new bomb to put in the sea. It was called a magnetic mine. The Germans dropped it from an aeroplane. It had a parachute. The magnetic mine lay on the sea bottom. It worked like a magnet when metal was near. When a ship sailed over the top the magnetic mine blew up. So did the ship.

Nazi troops parading through Warsaw, 1939.

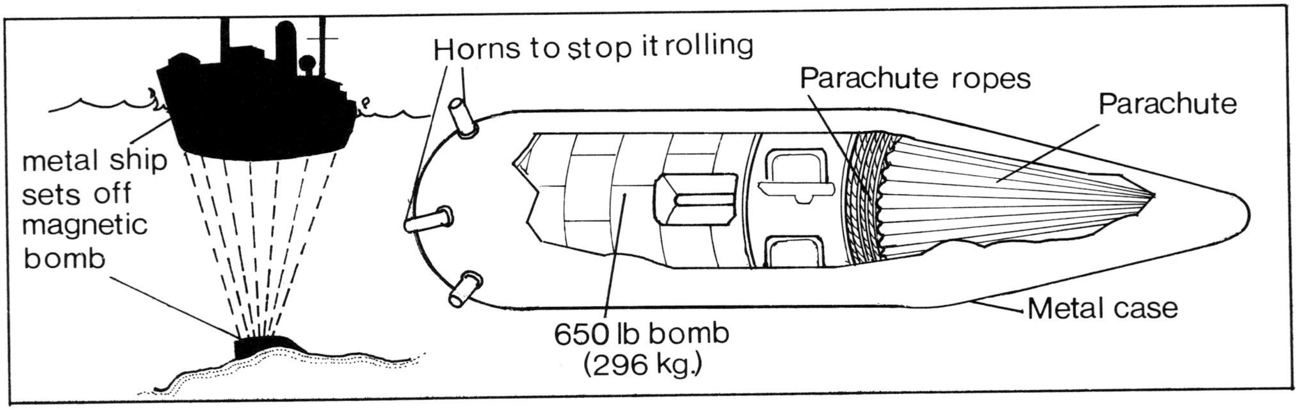

The German parachute magnetic mine.

The Germans had many submarines. These were called U-boats. Germany attacked all British ships. They also attacked all ships that were sailing to Britain. No one in a ship around Britain was safe. The ship *Athenia* was the first ship sunk. It was a passenger ship. It was sunk by a torpedo from U30.

Things to Do

1 Fill in the gaps. (*Numbers in brackets refer to text line numbers.*)
Poland was a long way from ——————— (1). Britain could not help Poland because Britain's ———— (3) was small. Britain did have a good ———— (8). This was not much help to Poland. The Germans bombed Poland's biggest city which was called ——————(22). Then they took over Poland. Next they tried to sink British ————— (34). They used U-boats and ————— (44) to blow up ships.

2 What was a U-boat?

3 GERMANY WANTED MORE LAND – 1940

Norway and Denmark taken by Germany

In April 1940 Germany wanted more land again. So Germany took Norway in April 1940. She also took Denmark.

Britain and France were very worried indeed. Germany was taking more and more land in Europe. She was moving closer and closer to Britain and France.

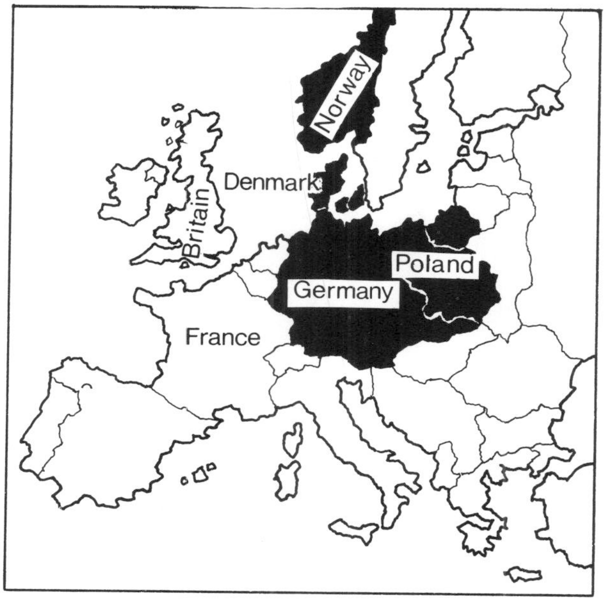

Germany taking more land.

A fort on the Belgian part of the Maginot Line, 1939.

The Maginot Line

France was ready to defend herself. She had built a line of forts. This was called the Maginot Line. It had deep ditches. It had concrete and steel forts and many large guns. The forts went deep underground. They would be safe from bombs. The French believed that the Germans could never break through this line. They spent a great deal of money to make it strong.

The Maginot Line ran along the border between France and Germany. It stopped at Luxembourg and Belgium.

The Germans decided not to fight against the Maginot Line. They would lose many men and tanks. So they decided to go round the Line. They attacked France by going through Belgium. Belgium tried to keep out of the war. She was a very small country. She knew she could not stand up to Germany or any other large country. She wanted to stay neutral. She did not really have a chance.

Blitzkreig

The Germans had thought up a new

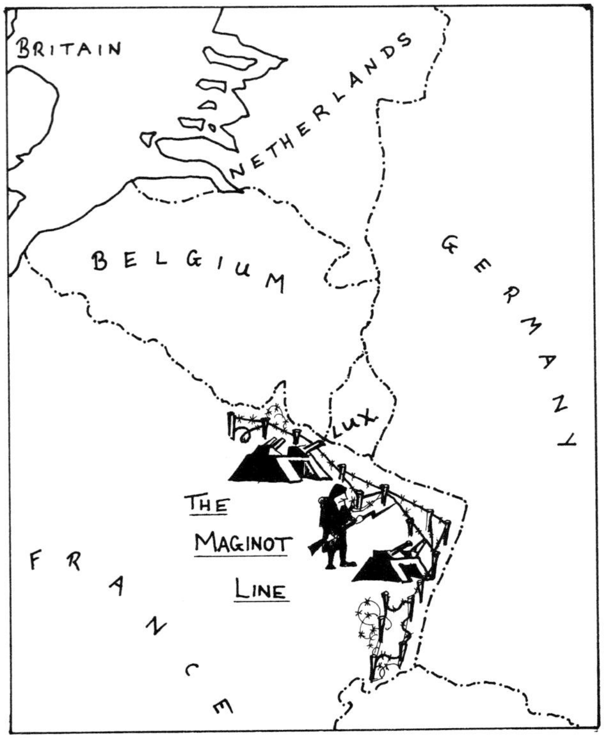

Where the Maginot Line was built.

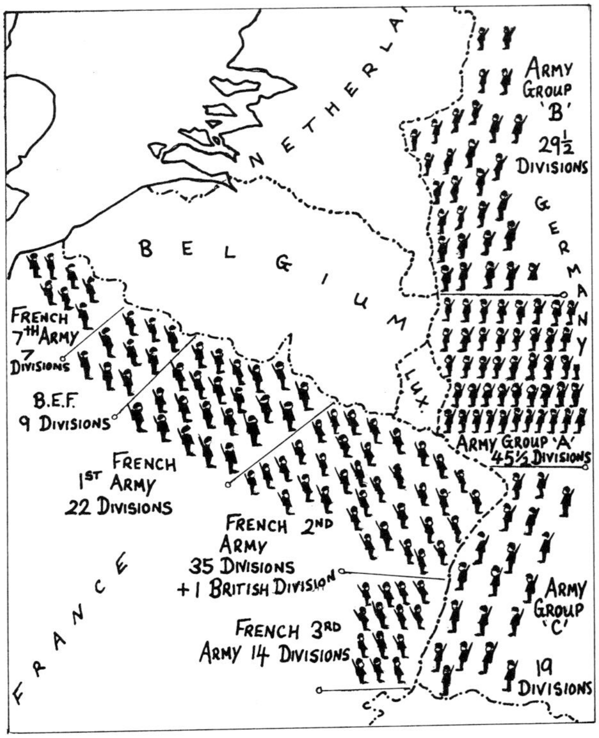

The two sides facing each other.

type of warfare. It was called *Blitzkrieg*. It meant lightning (or quick) war. This meant that they would use their fast armoured vehicles. They would rush through the enemy. Then the slower soldiers would follow. They would finish off the enemy.

The *Blitzkrieg* worked against Poland. Germany hoped it would work against France.

The Germans had 136 divisions. Most of these divisions were large groups of ordinary soldiers. These were called infantry divisions. Some of these divisions were soldiers with fast, armoured vehicles. These were called Panzer divisions.

The armies

The British and French had a large army too. Look at the figures. Which side do you think is the stronger?

Germany	*France and Britain*
136 divisions of soldiers	149 divisions of soldiers
2,700 armoured vehicles	3,000 armoured vehicles
2,000 bombers	4,000 bombers
1,500 fighters	1,000 fighters

Things to Do

1 Fill in the gaps. (*Numbers in brackets refer to text line numbers.*)
Germany took Norway in April ———— (2). Then Germany turned on France. France had a line of forts called the ———————— (10) Line. The ———————— (26) went round the Line. The Germans moved very fast. They had ——— (48) divisions of soldiers. The British and French had ——— (58) divisions.

2 Why could Belgium not stand up to Germany?

4 GERMANY ATTACKED FRANCE

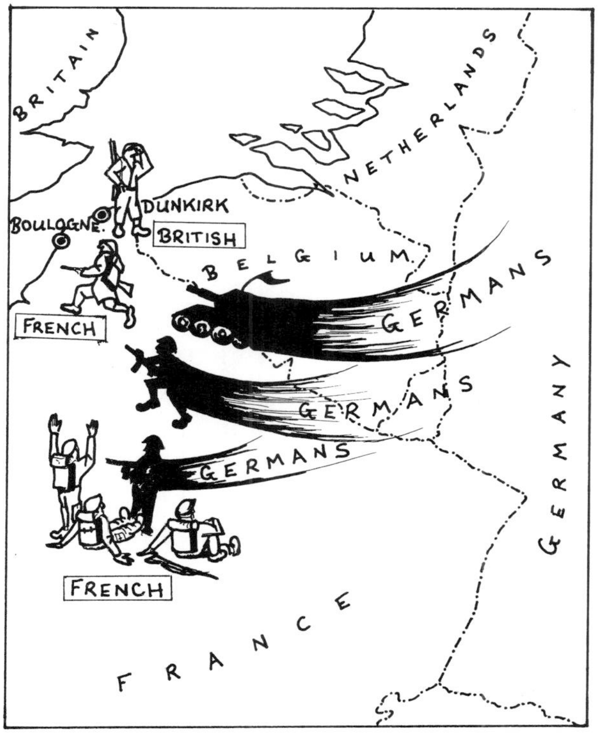

The retreat to Dunkirk.

Retreating soldiers and refugees taking cover in a ditch during an enemy air attack on a main road.

Germany attacked France. She started on 10 May 1940. The Germans cut the British and French armies in half and pushed them back. They reached Boulogne on 20 May.

The British and French retreat to Dunkirk.

The French and British were in trouble. Many of their soldiers were trapped. The British decided that they must escape. They retreated to Dunkirk.

Sergeant Upton was in the 124th Field Service Regiment of the Royal Artillery. They were driving slowly, in lorries, towards Dunkirk. The roads were jammed with soldiers, lorries, carts, bicycles and cars. Thousands of people were running away from the Germans. It was like a bad dream.

Sergeant Upton and his men made their way to a place called Fletre. It was 20 miles from Dunkirk. Upton went forward to find out what they should do next. His commanding officer said, 'The war's over for you fellows. We've got to get back to England. Leave the lorries and tanks and march the men to Dunkirk. Be quick about it.'

Some of the tiny boats which took part in the evacuation from Dunkirk being towed up the River Thames for repair shortly afterwards.

Boats were needed

What would happen when they reached Dunkirk? Boats were needed to take the soldiers back to Britain. Somebody had to gather the boats together. Admiral Ramsay was given the job. He worked hard. Large ships were needed. They would bring hundreds of soldiers home to Britain. The port of Dunkirk had been badly bombed. Few ships could use it. Large ships could not sail right up to the beaches. The water was too shallow.

Many small boats were needed. Eight hundred and sixty small boats were gathered together. There were all sorts. There were barges. Many of the barges were river boats. They were not really strong enough for going to sea. There were pleasure boats from rivers. There were cargo boats. There were tugs that towed lifeboats.

The small boats all sailed together to Dunkirk. When they reached Dunkirk they sailed right up to the beaches. The soldiers waded out. Often the water was up to their armpits. They scrambled aboard and crouched down. The boats picked up as many soldiers as they could carry. When they were full they were rowed out to the large ships. The soldiers were helped aboard the large ships. As many soldiers as possible were crammed in. They sat and lay all over the decks. They were tired out. Then the small boats sailed back to the beaches for more soldiers.

Men lined up on the beach at Dunkirk waiting to be rescued.

'Sunset at Dunkirk'—a drawing made by an artist who was there. Junkers dive-bombers are attacking shipping and a paddle-steamer has been hit and beached.

The beaches of Dunkirk

The beaches of Dunkirk were huge and sandy. Thousands of soldiers stood on the beaches. They were waiting to go to the large ships. The soldiers were in groups of fifty. When it was their turn to go they were called through a loud hailer.

All these soldiers had to be fed. There was no food in Dunkirk. There was no clean water to drink. Food and water had to be brought from Britain. The Germans bombed Dunkirk all the time. Ships came in bringing food. Ships went out taking soldiers home to Britain. Aeroplanes fought and screamed overhead. Great fires burnt. The oil tanks at Dunkirk had been set on fire. Bombs whizzed down. They thudded into the sand. The bombs were not as bad as they sounded. At first, the soldiers were very scared. Thousands of soldiers waited on the wide beaches. A bomb could kill hundreds. But it didn't. One soldier said, 'If ever I'm bombed again, give me a sandy beach. The bomb sinks into the sand. Only a few men are hurt each time.'

Danger to ships

Over 300,000 soldiers were brought back to Britain. Find out how many people are in your school. You can then work out how many schools would have been taken off at Dunkirk. Many ships were badly damaged.

Many ships sank. The wrecks stuck up out of the water. Other ships ran into them and sank too. It was very dangerous.

It was very lucky that the weather was fine. Fine weather meant that the sea was calm. It was easier to load the boats.

All sorts of things happened. Many soldiers had to wade out into deep water. Some had to swim. They found that their greatcoats soaked up the

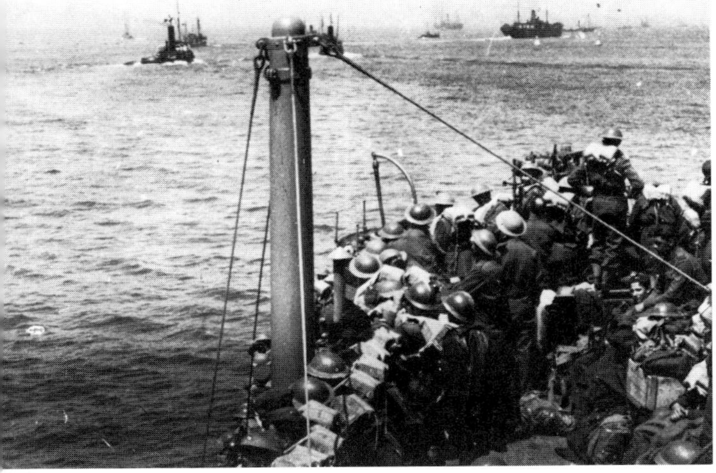

Ships leaving Dunkirk for England.

Men on board a ship leaving Dunkirk. How many different expressions can you see on their faces? What is the most common expression? Why do you think that is? How do you know the soldiers are British?

water. They were too heavy and dragged them down. They took their greatcoats off. Then they dropped them in the water. Hundreds of coats were floating around. They got round the propellers of the small boats. It could take a long time to get the coats off the propeller.

The work of rescuing all the British and French soldiers began on 27 May. It went on for nine days. The last soldiers were taken off on 4 June. The last ship to leave Dunkirk was the *Princess Maud*. She sailed away at 1.50 a.m.

The rearguard

Several thousand British and French soldiers stayed behind. These were the soldiers known as the rearguard. They stayed to fight off the Germans so that the rest could get away. At nine o'clock in the morning they gave up.

All the British and French soldiers in the rearguard were sent to prisoner of war camps. Most of them stayed there for the rest of the war. They could feel proud, however. They had saved the biggest part of the British army. They had also saved many French soldiers. All these soldiers were saved to fight another day. They did fight again. Later in the war they fought to defeat Germany.

Some things were not saved. All the tanks and lorries and heavy guns had to be left behind at Dunkirk. There was no room for them on the ships.

Vehicles and dead left behind at Dunkirk.

Things to Do

1 Why were large ships needed?
2 Why were small ships needed?
3 Why were the soldiers glad that the beaches were sandy?
4 Why did the soldiers take off their greatcoats?
5 What did the rearguard do?
6 Do the crossword.

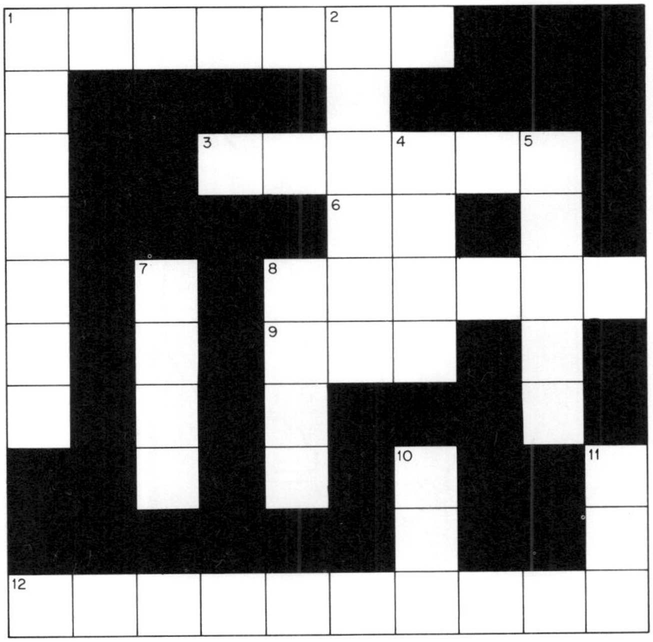

Numbers in brackets after some clues refer to text line numbers.

ACROSS

1 'They retreated to ————————.' (9)
3 'The roads were ——————— with soldiers, lorries, carts, bicycles and cars.' (14)
6 'They stayed to fight off the Germans —— that the rest could get away.' (134)
8 'Many of the —————— were river boats.' (46)
9 Old word for yes.
12 'They took their —————————— off.' (117)

DOWN

1 'They were ———————— slowly, in lorries, towards Dunkirk.' (13)
2 'Admiral —————— was given the job.' (34)
4 Opposite of less.
5 'It was like a bad —————.' (18)
7 'There were ———— that towed lifeboats.' (51)
8 'Then the small boats sailed ———— to the beaches for more soldiers.' (67)
10 'Other ships ran into them and sank ———.' (105)
11 'When it ——— their turn to go they were called through a loud hailer.' (73)

5 WILL THE GERMANS INVADE?

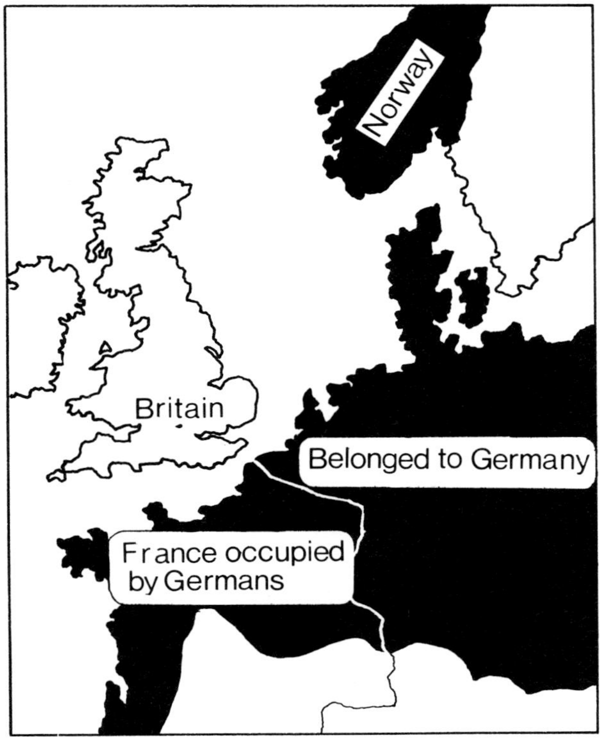

France occupied by Germany.

Germany took over France

The British army escaped from Dunkirk in June 1940. Some of the French soldiers went with them. When they had all gone the Germans took over France. The Germans occupied all the parts of France they wanted. French people went on living there, but the Germans ruled.

Germany wanted Britain to make peace but Britain would not. The Germans decided that they must knock Britain out of the war. It was too dangerous to leave her alone. Britain was weak but she would become stronger. When Britain was stronger she might attack Germany.

Germany decided to invade Britain

The Germans decided to invade Britain. It was a difficult job. Britain is surrounded by sea. Many boats and ships were needed to take the German soldiers to Britain. All these boats had to be collected together in France. Then the Germans had to work out the best time to invade. The weather had to be good. The tide had to be right. There were two good dates. One date was 19 September. The other good date was 27 September. The weather forecast for the last half of September was bad. However, the Germans could not

Where the Germans planned to land in Britain.

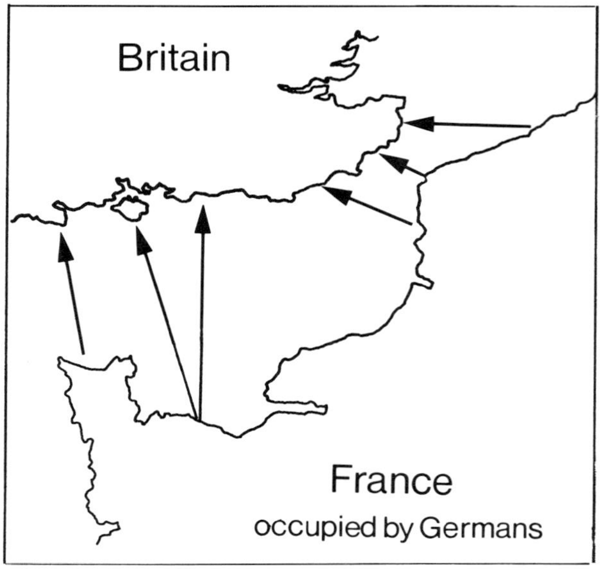

leave the invasion until winter.

They planned to make six landings in Britain.

Britain's air force

There was one problem that was bigger than all the others. The problem was Britain's air force. The Germans had to destroy Britain's air force. This was because ships can easily be bombed by aeroplanes. If the Germans were sailing their ships across to Britain, the British could easily bomb the ships. The German ships and soldiers would be destroyed. The Germans knew that they must destroy Britain's air force. The job of destroying Britain's air force was given to the Luftwaffe. The Luftwaffe was the name for the German air force.

Things to Do

1 Fill in the gaps. (*Numbers in brackets refer to text line numbers.*)
The Germans took over France. They decided to invade –––––––– (17). They needed many boats. This was because Britain is surrounded by ––– (18). The weather had to be –––– (25). They also needed the right tide. There were ––– (26) good dates. Both were in the month of –––––––––– (27). First of all the German air force had to destroy Britain's ––– –––––– (37).

2 Why did the Germans decide that they must knock Britain out of the war?

3 Why did the Germans have to destroy Britain's air force?

4 What was the name of the German air force?

Part of Britain's airforce—some fighter planes.

6 THE LUFTWAFFE – THE GERMAN AIR FORCE

The German air force was called the Luftwaffe. It was very large and efficient. The numbers of German aeroplanes are listed here:

Long range bombers (these are slow heavy planes)	1,180
Dive bombers	400
Fighters (these are fast aeroplanes for protecting bombers)	1,180

The Germans had well over twice as many aeroplanes as the British had.

Diagram showing all the people needed to keep a bomber in the air. How many men flew the bomber? Why was the weather man important? What do you think the job of the flying control man was?

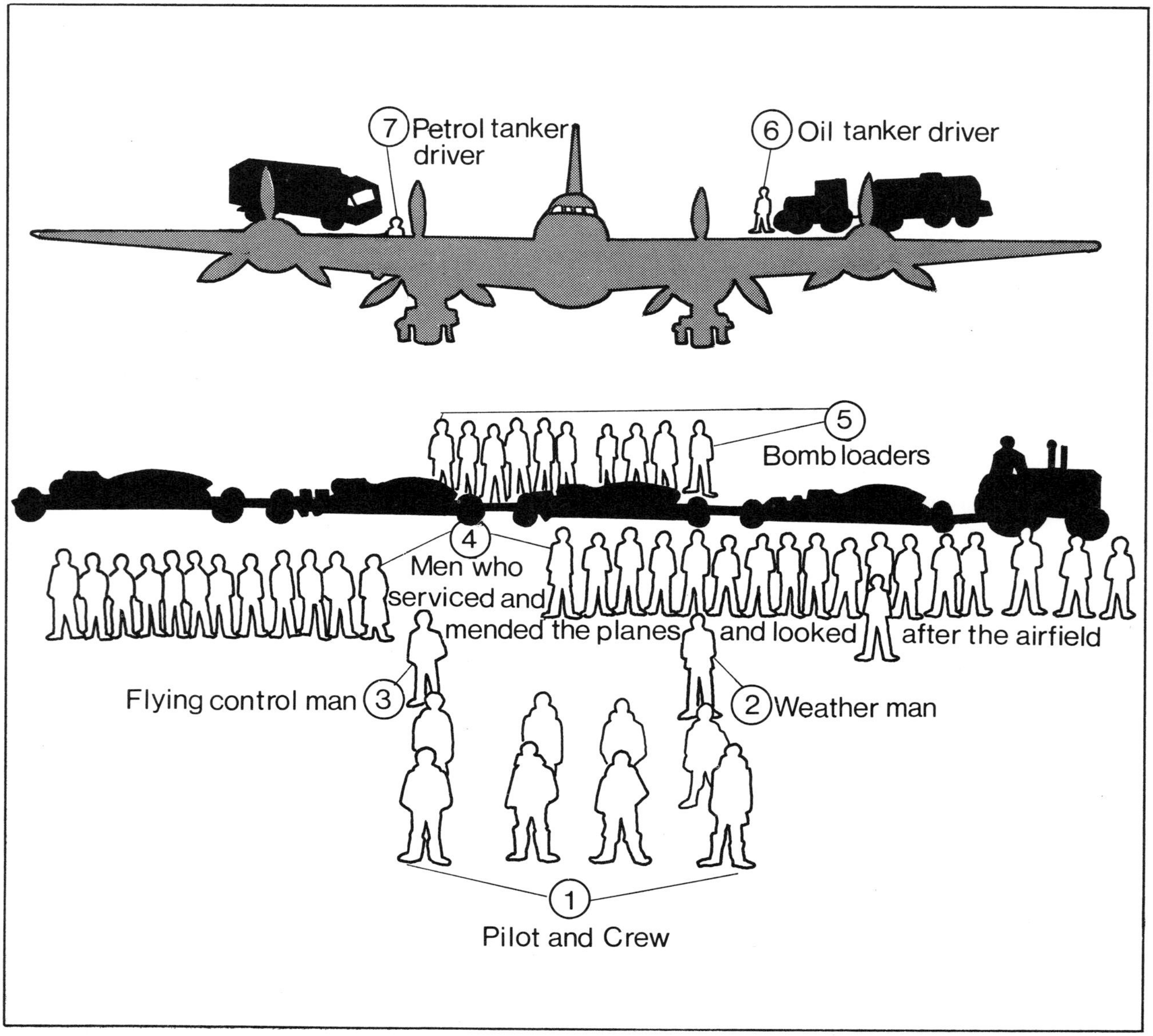

These are some of the most important German aeroplanes. The Heinkel He111 was slow and was easily caught by British fighters. The Dornier DO 17 was known as the flying pencil. The Junkers JU88 was the most successful bomber. It could be used in all sorts of ways. It worked as a dive bomber, mine layer, ordinary bomber or fighter plane. The Messerschmitt BF109E was the most important German fighter plane.

German pilots

Aeroplanes are very important in air battles. Pilots are also important. The German pilots were well trained and brave. So were the men who made up the crew on a bomber. The German air force was well organised. It took a large number of men to keep planes flying. It took far more men than just the pilot and his crew. Look at the diagram showing roughly how many men it took to keep a large bomber (British or German) in the air. This is not counting the men who built the plane.

The German air force was divided into groups. These were called airfleets. Three airfleets were ready to attack Britain. They were ready to attack the places that built ships and made guns.

The German air force ready to attack Britain.

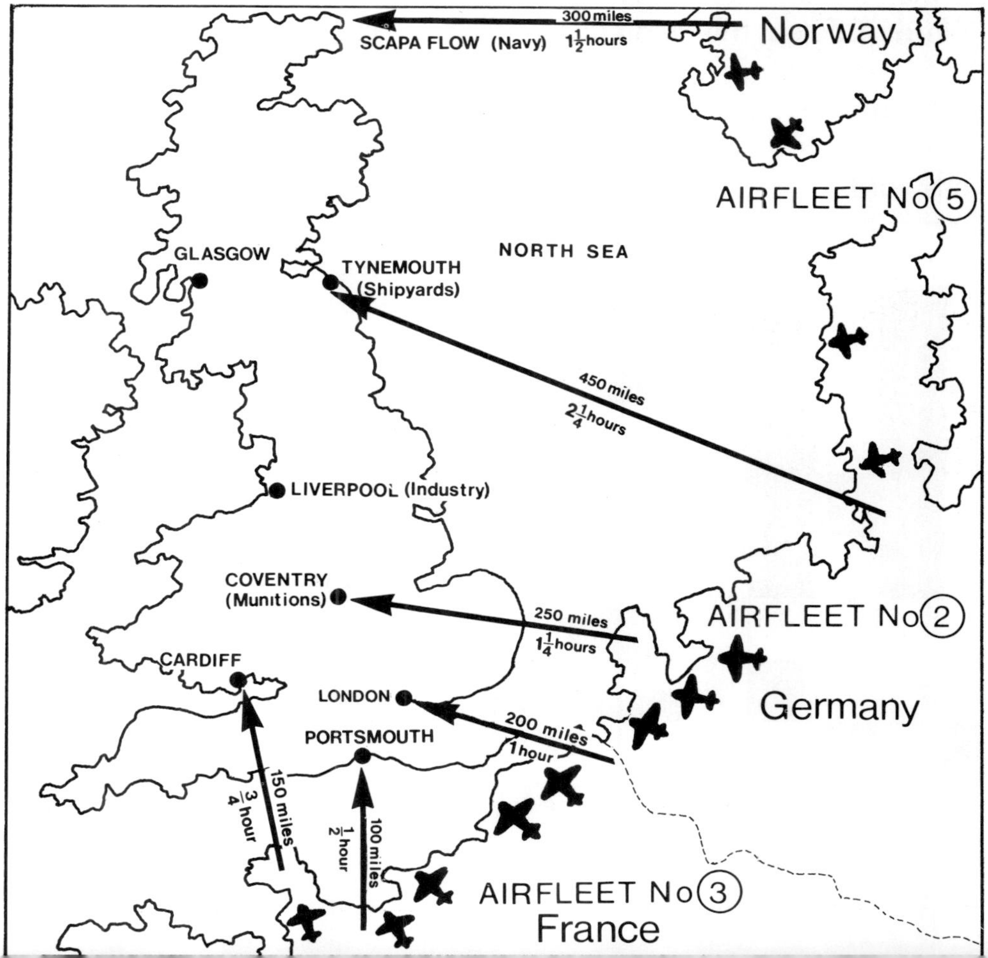

German pilots' badge. Draw this in your book.

Things to Do

1 Fill in the gaps. (*Numbers in brackets refer to text line numbers.*)
The Germans had ––––– (5) long range bombers. They had ––––– (8) fighters. They had ––– (7) dive bombers. The ––––––––––––––– BF109E (23) was the most important German fighter plane. Aeroplanes were expensive and difficult to fly. This meant that ––––––– (29) had to be well trained and brave.

2 How many men did it take to keep a bomber flying? (Look at the diagram on page 16.)

3 How many German airfleets were ready to attack Britain?

4 Do the crossword.

Numbers in brackets after some clues refer to text line numbers.

ACROSS

1 'The German air force was called the ––––––––––.' (1)
6 Opposite of no.
7 Opposite of short.
9 '–– took a large number of men to keep planes flying.' (33)
11 Word meaning to talk in a friendly way.
12 'The –––––––– DO17, was known as the flying pencil.' (17)
14 Boy child.
15 'The Germans had well over –––––– as many aeroplanes as the British had.' (11)
17 'It worked as a dive bomber, mine –––––, ordinary bomber or fighter plane.' (22)

DOWN

1 '–––– range bombers (these are slow heavy planes).' (5)
2 '–––––––– (these are fast aeroplanes for protecting bombers).' (8)
3 'It could be used in all sorts of ––––.' (20)
4 'Fighters (these are –––– aeroplanes for protecting bombers).' (8)
5 'The German ––––––– were well trained and brave.' (29)
8 A type of tree.
10 A metal can with food in it.
11 'So were the men who made up the –––– on a bomber.' (30)
13 The part of your face that you breathe through.
16 '–– was very large and efficient.' (2)

7 THE R.A.F. – THE BRITISH AIR FORCE

R.A.F. badge. Draw this in your book.

The British air force is called the Royal Air Force. It is known as the R.A.F. for short.

After France gave up, Britain was fighting Germany alone. The Germans were 'on the doorstep'. It was terrifying. However, Britain had known for a long time that she might be attacked. It was a shock to find the Germans so close but Britain was quite well prepared in some ways.

The British aeroplanes are listed here. This is roughly how many Britain had:

Bombers	530
Fighters	650

The fighters were very important. It was the fighters that had to keep out the German bombers.

The Spitfire was the most famous British fighter plane. It could accelerate very fast. It was quick and light to turn. The Hurricane was the other important fighter. It was very

Cutaway diagram of a Spitfire. How did the pilot get in? What sort of engine did the Spitfire have? What do you think the pilots meant when they said the fuel tank was in a dangerous place? How many machine guns were in the wing?

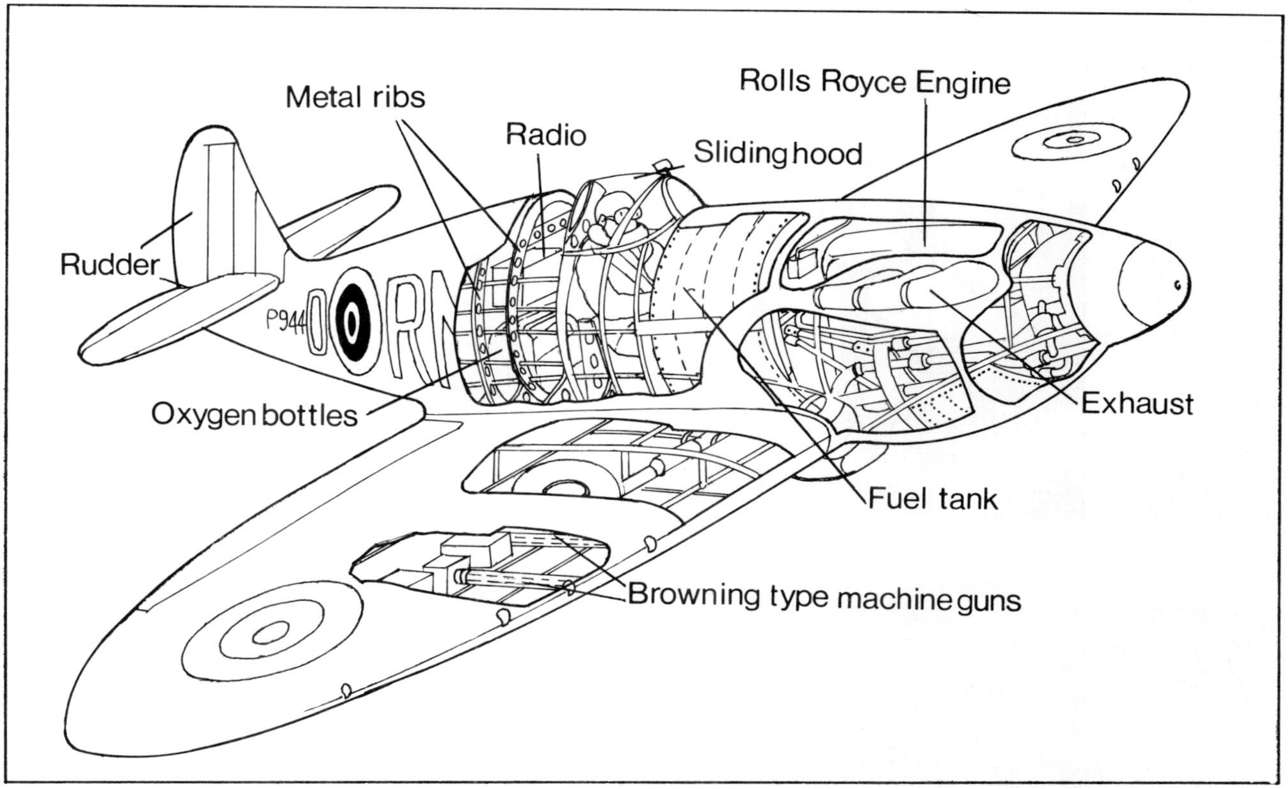

tough. It could take a great deal of damage. It was slow to accelerate and climb.

British pilots

The pilots were as important as the aeroplanes. Aeroplanes were very expensive. They were very complicated. They had to be flown well. Every time there was a crash, Britain lost an aeroplane. In 1940, Britain did not have enough aeroplanes. Therefore, each aeroplane was looked after carefully.

Frank Webster, a Spitfire pilot in flying gear. He finished his training in July 1940 and was killed in action on 26 August 1940.

Britain had to look after her pilots too. There were not enough pilots either. The R.A.F. trained its pilots very well.

There was also a Royal Auxiliary Air Force. This was started in 1925. There was the Royal Air Force Volunteer Reserve as well. These men had learnt to fly for fun. When war came in 1939 they became full-time pilots.

Foreign pilots

Many of the pilots flying in Britain were foreigners. There were volunteers from New Zealand, Canada, Australia and South Africa. There were a few Americans. There were Czechs, Poles, Norwegians, Dutch, Belgians and French.

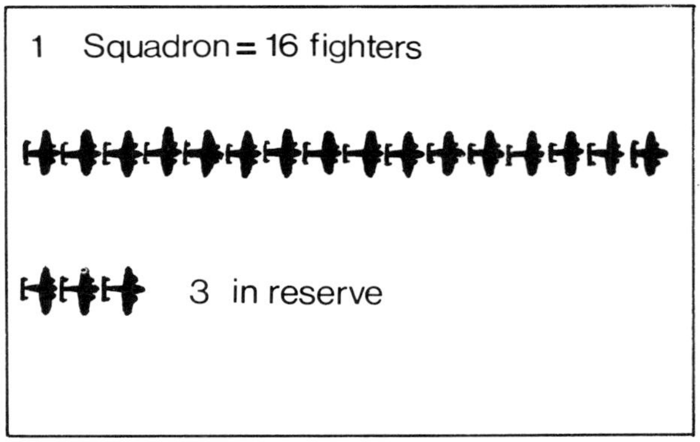

Squadrons, groups and airfields

All pilots belonged to squadrons. There were fifty-five squadrons of fighters in Britain. These squadrons were put in different parts of Britain. The different parts were called groups. The most important groups

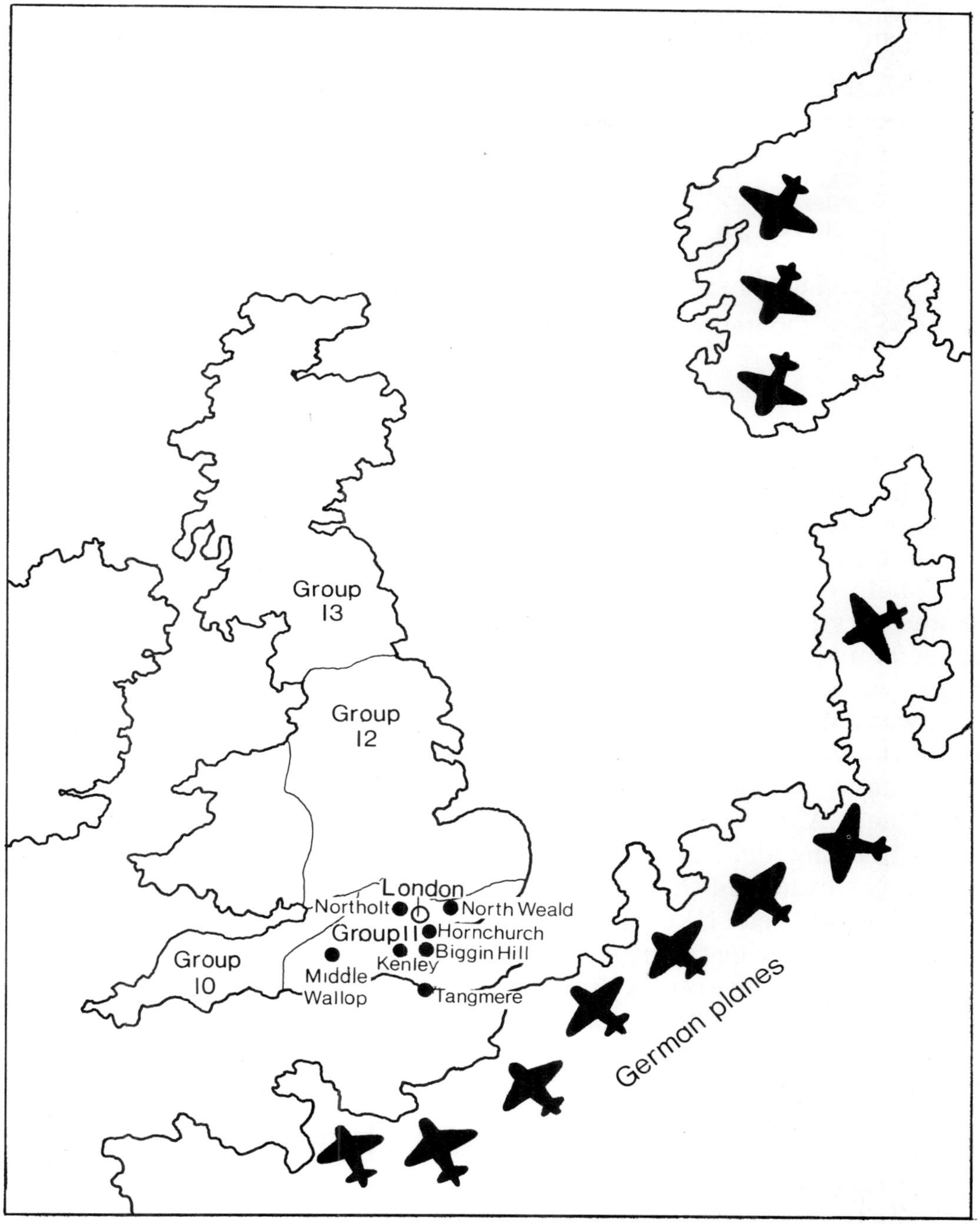

Fighter Command Groups.

were 10, 11, 12 and 13. Look at the map. Which was the most important of the four groups and why?

Each group had important airfields. These were called sector airfields. The sector airfields controlled smaller airfields. All airfields were linked by radio.

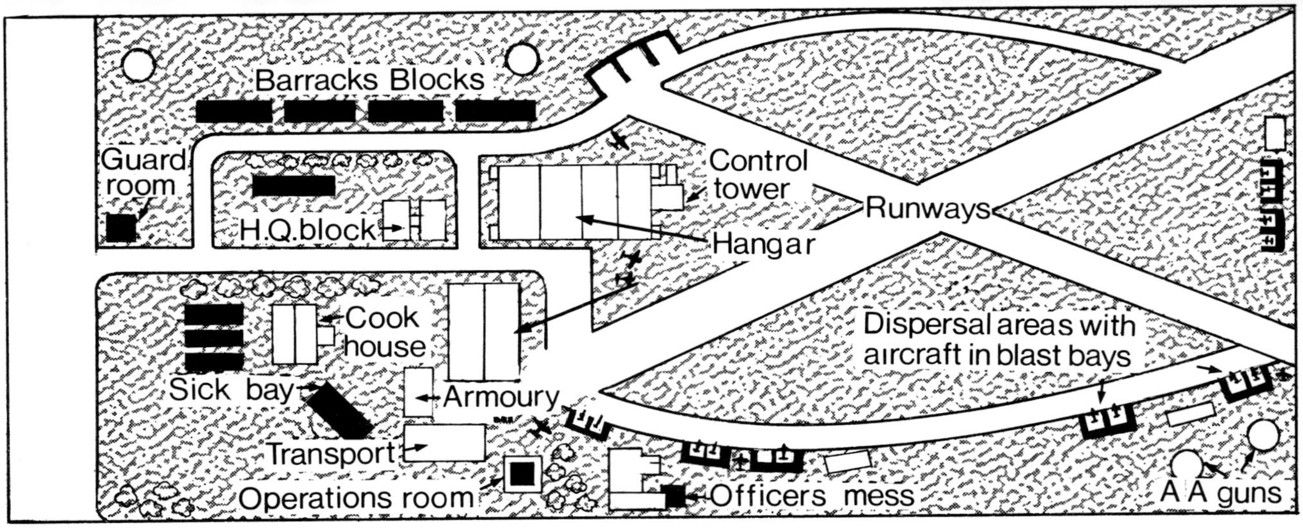

Plan of an R.A.F. sector airfield.

Radar

Britain had one great advantage. It was radar. Radar meant that Britain knew that German bombers were coming before they could be seen. This was very important. The R.A.F. could send up its fighters to catch the bombers when the bombers were still miles away. Many radar stations were built around Britain. The radar stations gave their messages to the R.A.F. The R.A.F. ordered the fighters into the air. They told them where they would find the bombers. The order would read like this: 'Bandit flying at over twenty thousand feet, in the area of Smith's Knoll lightship. Climb to angels twenty-five on a heading 040 degrees.'

Bandit=a German bomber. Angels=height. Degrees=direction.

The R.A.F. pilots would run to their fighters, leap in and set off to attack the bombers. They wanted to drive the bombers away before they could drop their bombs. The bombers might change the direction they were going in. The R.A.F. fighter pilots would be told about this on their radio.

Radar.

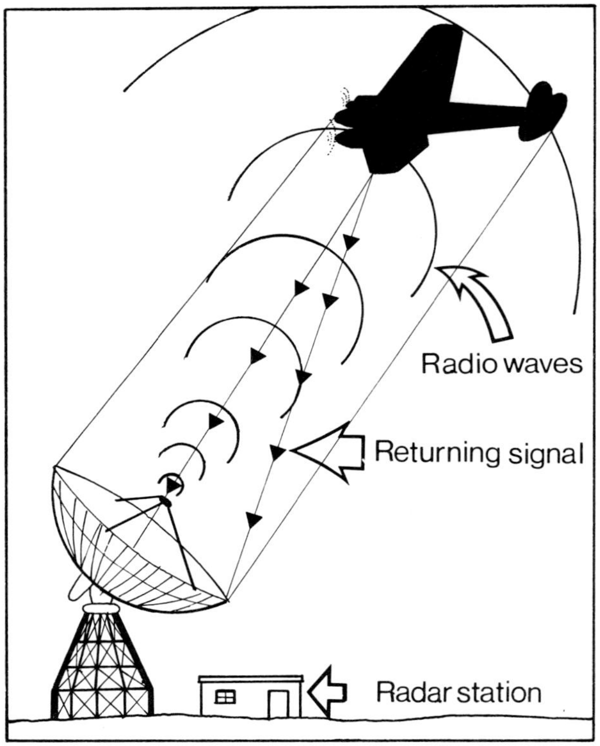

All the radar stations faced the sea. Radar could not see planes already over Britain. So look-outs were used. They were people who watched for German aeroplanes. Then they rang the R.A.F. They told them how many German aeroplanes there were. They said where the aeroplanes were heading.

German bombers coming in to attack.

Barrage balloons and anti-aircraft guns

Huge silver-coloured balloons were used. They were to stop German bombers flying low. They were called barrage balloons.

A barrage balloon being raised over the Tower of London.

Anti-aircraft guns in action at night.

Anti-aircraft guns were everywhere. They were known as AA guns. There were AA guns all round Britain's coasts. There were also AA guns at fighter airfields and in cities.

Things to Do

1 Fill in the gaps. (*Numbers in brackets refer to text line numbers.*)
The British air force is called the ----- --- ------ (2). The two most important British fighters were the --------- and the ---------- (20). Britain knew when the German bombers were coming. This was because Britain had ------ (70).
2 Which fighter—the Spitfire or the Hurricane— would a pilot enjoy flying most, and why, do you think?
3 What did the sector airfields do?
4 What were barrage balloons for?

8 THE BATTLE OF BRITAIN

PART 1

A fight over the Channel.

The Battle of Britain began on 10 July and ended on 31 October 1940. The date when the Battle of Britain is celebrated is 15 September.

10 July

It was an exciting and frightening time. On 10 July the weather was not good. Before breakfast some British fighters were guarding some ships. Two German bombers came in to attack. The British fighters were Hurricanes. They drove off the bombers.

The race to win the war was on. The Battle of Britain had begun. The afternoon came. A large number of ships were sailing along the narrow part of the English Channel. Six Hurricanes were guarding them. The radar stations were keeping a look-out. They reported many German bombers around Calais in France. Four squadrons of British fighters took off (a squadron had sixteen planes). They were told to go to the ships. More joined them from the airfield at Kenley.

Twenty German bombers attacked the ships. The German bombers were guarded by their own fighters. The six Hurricanes did what they could. Then, suddenly the four squadrons of British fighters arrived. The sky became a mass of plunging aircraft. Three Hurricanes were shot down. Five German fighters were shot down. Only one small ship was sunk. The German bombers were driven off.

'Scramble!'

Day after day the air battles went on. Britain's pilots were on duty without a break. If the German air force destroyed the R.A.F. Britain would be invaded. The pilots knew this. They fought hard and desperately. Every time they flew it was called a

Pilots running to their Hurricanes during the Battle of Britain.

sortie. Pilots made sortie after sortie. They landed their fighters. They had them refuelled. Then they took off again. The pilots slept in their flying clothes. They were ready to go at any moment. The weather turned fine. They spent spare hours lying on the grass in the shade of the trees. A telephone would ring. The message would come over, 'SCRAMBLE!' They leapt to their feet and ran to the planes. They would strap on their parachutes as they ran. In two minutes they took off. They might return in a few hours. They would eat a quick snack and take off again.

R.A.F. air crew having a snack between flying duties, 1940.

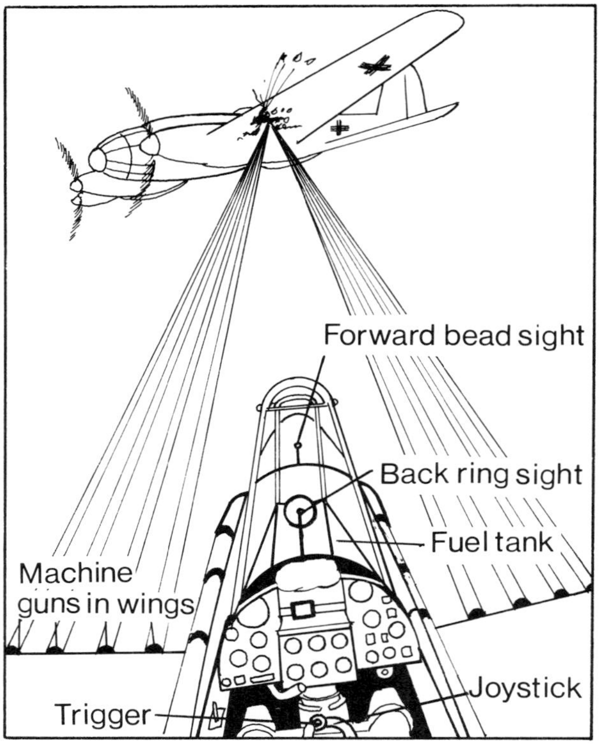

Machine gun fire from a fighter shooting down an enemy plane. What do you think the sights were for?

Fighting and dying

Many pilots did not come back. They were unlucky. The lucky ones became very good pilots. They learnt a great deal about air fighting. This helped them to stay alive.

Wing Commander 'Sailor' Malan was a famous Battle of Britain pilot. He drew up the rules for air fighting given in the poster.

When a plane crashed there was not much left of the pilot. This is a verse from a funny but sad song called *The Dying Airman*:

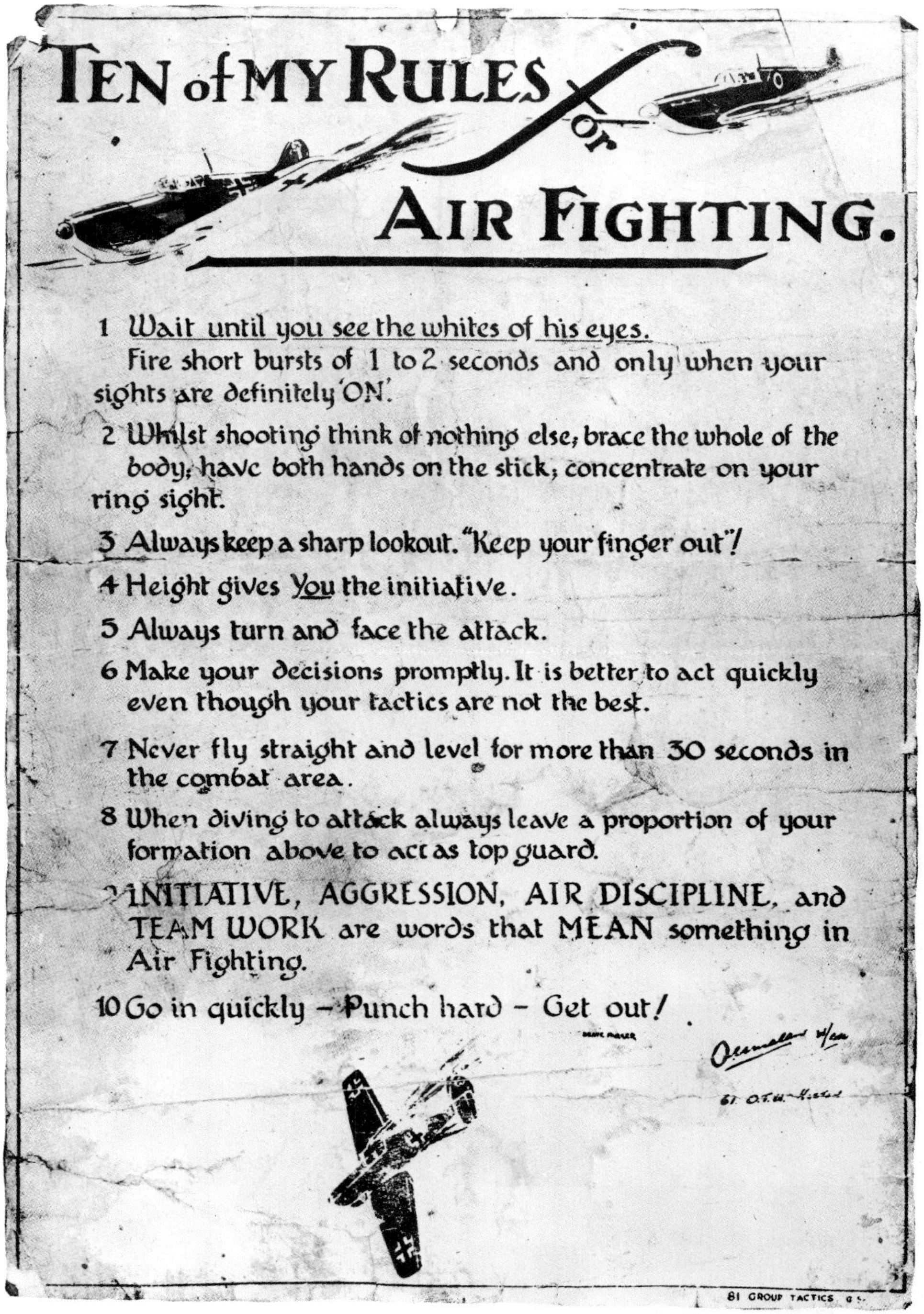

Two valve springs you'll find in my stomach,
Three spark plugs are safe in my lung,
The prop is in splinters inside me,
To my fingers the joystick has clung.

The most usual death for a pilot was by burning. The fuel tanks were close to the cockpit.

Things to Do

1 Fill in the gaps. (*Numbers in brackets refer to text line numbers.*)
The Battle of Britain ended on 31 ———————— (1). Pilots fought hard. ————— (67) Commander 'Sailor' Malan Wrote out some rules for ——— (69) fighting. The rules are given in the ——————— (70). The pilots were very brave. They knew that any day they might die. The most usual way to die was by ———————— (82).
2 Write out rule no. 10 of Malan's rules.
3 Discuss 'Ten of My Rules for Air Fighting'. What do you think no. 1 means? Which do you think is the most important rule? What is the reasoning behind no. 7?
4 Do the crossword.

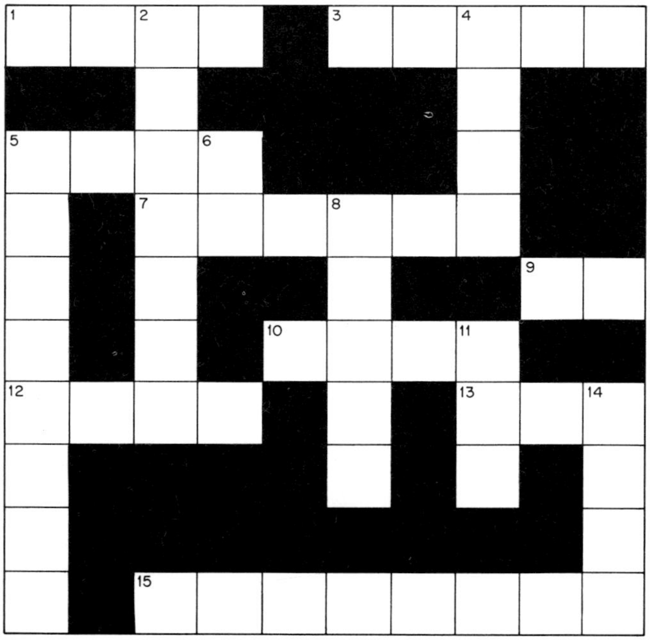

Numbers in brackets after some clues refer to the text line numbers.

ACROSS
1 'The Battle of Britain began on 10 ————'. (1)
3 'They —————— off the bombers.' (11)
5 Opposite of fast.
7 'More joined them from the airfield at ———————.' (25)
9 Short for anti-aircraft.
10 '———— German fighters were shot down.' (35)
12 'The ———— when the Battle of Britain is celebrated is 15 September.' (3)
13 'Day after day the ——— battles went on.' (38)
15 'The message would come over, —————————!' (53)

DOWN
2 'The radar stations were keeping a ———— ———.' (18)
4 '———— one small ship was sunk.' (36)
5 '(a ————————— had sixteen planes.)' (23)
6 You and me together.
8 'They spent spare hours —————— on the grass in the shade of the trees.' (51)
11 'They would ——— a quick snack and take off again.' (60)
14 'The ———— to win the war was on.' (13)

9 THE BATTLE OF BRITAIN

PART 2

Bombing airfields and aircraft factories

In August, Hitler gave the following order: 'The German Air Force is to overpower the British air force (R.A.F.) with all the forces at its command in the shortest possible time.'

He said that the airfields must be bombed so that no planes could use them. He also said that factories making aircraft must be bombed. Anything to do with the R.A.F. had to be destroyed. It had to be destroyed quickly.

On 12 August the Germans attacked in great numbers. They started by pretending to attack. They drew the British fighters in to attack them. Then they rushed other bombers in to attack the airfields. The Germans also attacked the radar stations. They had realised how important radar was. British hearts sank. If the radar stations were knocked out how long could the

R.A.F. fighter pilots and their equipment.
1. Why would boots be dangerous if a pilot came down in the sea?
2.What was the life jacket for?
3. Why do you think that a bulky flying jacket could be a nuisance for a pilot?
4. Why do you think a fighter pilot would get neckache?
5. Many fighter pilots, who wore a flying jacket, cut the collar off. Why do you think they did this?

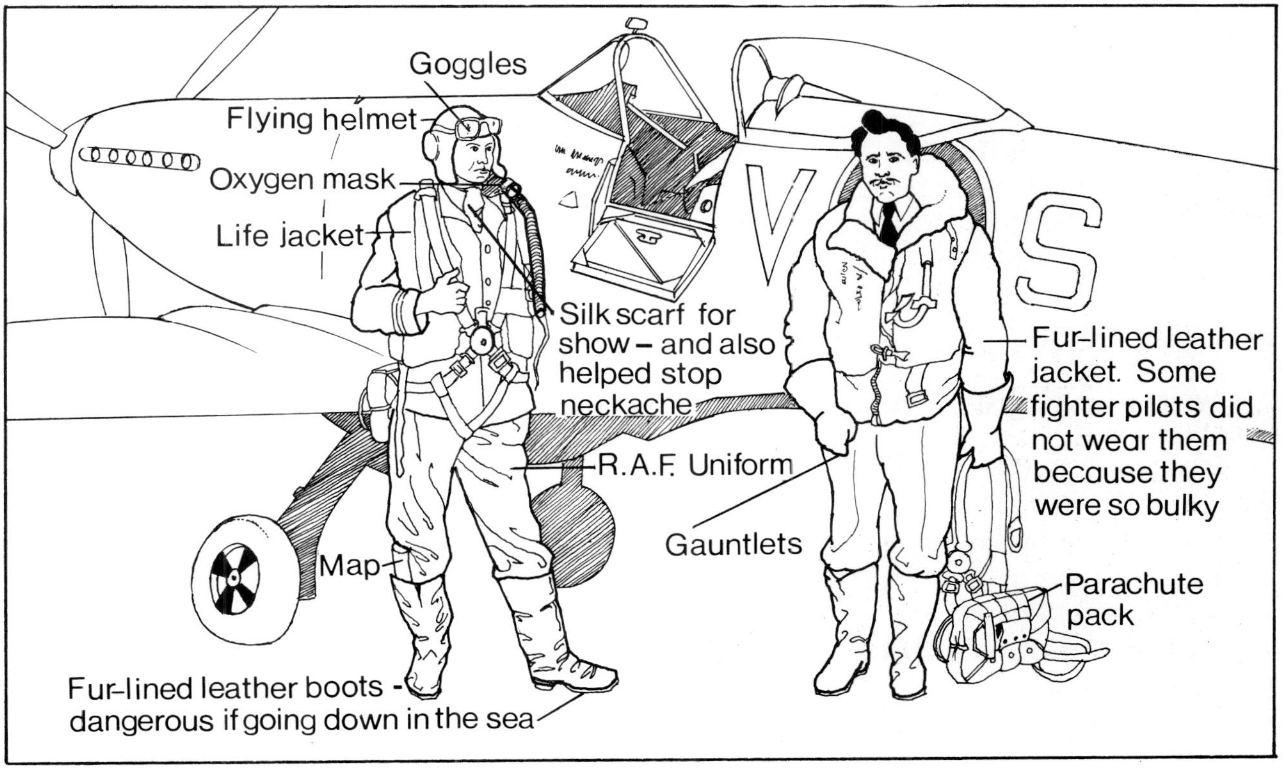

German bomber over London.

fighters keep going?

Luckily the damage was not very bad. Radar stations were difficult to bomb. It was hard to damage them badly.

13 August

The next day was 13 August. The Germans made the hardest attacks so far. They started at 6 o'clock in the morning. They sent over 200 aeroplanes. Luckily nearly all the radar stations were working again; 120 fighters were sent up to meet the German planes. Later in the morning there was another attack. Again it hit at the airfields. All the attacks were huge. This is how one Canadian pilot saw it:

> The air was filled with Nazi aircraft. There seemed to be thousands of Messerschmitts, Spitfires and Hurricanes all mixed up in dog-fights. I climbed up to 15,000 feet and saw a Messerschmitt chasing a Hurricane. I dived down on its tail to sea level. He zoomed up to 5,000 feet. I followed and after my first burst of fire he blew up in the air. I watched pieces of flaming aircraft dive into the sea.

Night bombing and the ***Knickebein***

By the end of the day the men in the R.A.F. were exhausted. But the attacks did not stop. German bombers bombed aircraft factories in the night. They were not very successful. It was difficult to find the factories in the dark. The Germans had a special radio beam. The radio beam was sent out from Germany. It pointed to the place to be bombed. All the bomber had to do was fly along the beam. It was called the *Knickebein* beacon. The British found out about this. They worked very hard to learn all about it. They learnt to jam the beam. They could move the beam around. This meant they could stop German bombers dropping their bombs on factories.

This was a good thing but it was not going to win the Battle of Britain. For two weeks the Germans

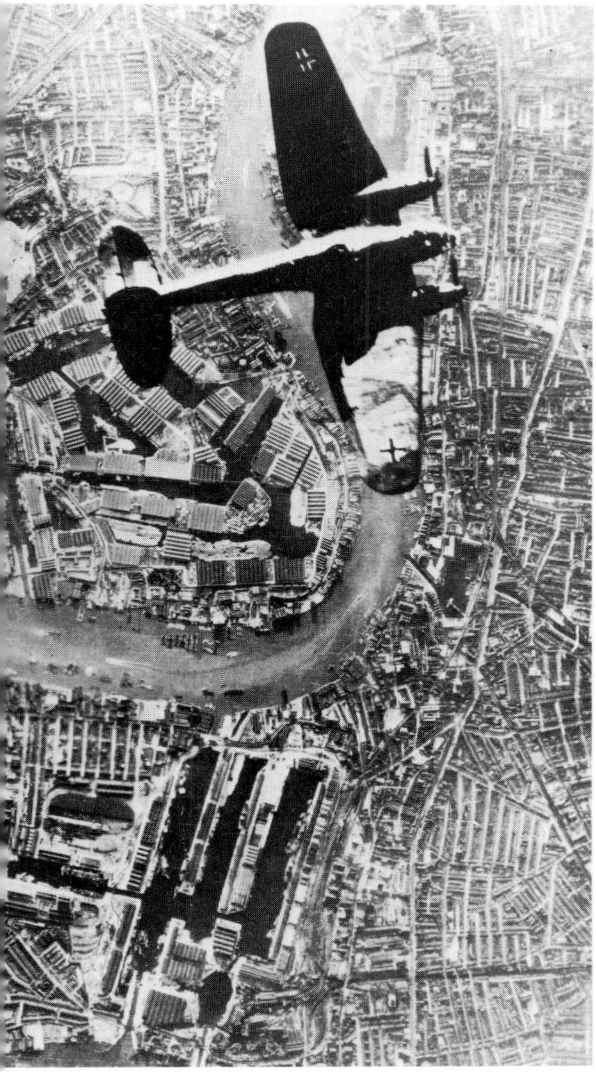

attacked again and again. Could the British hold on? Some people almost despaired.

The biggest German attack yet

On 15 August came the biggest German attack yet. The Germans attacked in the north of England. They attacked in the south and in the west. They seemed to be everywhere. All day long, fights between aeroplanes went on in the sunny skies.

Britain running out of planes and pilots

On 18 August both sides counted their losses for that day. The Germans had lost 71 planes. The British had lost 27. The British were pleased but they still had a great deal to worry about. There were two grim facts. Firstly, about 350 new fighter pilots were needed in the next week. There were only 80 ready. Secondly, 213 fighters had been lost in the last week. Only 150 new fighters had been built. Britain could not go on having fighters and their pilots destroyed. She had not got enough as it was. Her supply was running out. On the other hand, the Germans had plenty of pilots and planes. They could go on fighting for a long time.

Sector airfields

The Germans had found out that some airfields were more important than others. The most important ones were the sector airfields. They controlled all the other airfields. The most famous of the sector airfields were Biggin Hill and Hornchurch. They were both badly bombed. The runways were bombed. The fighters were bombed on the ground. There were seven sector stations in all. Six of them were seriously damaged. This was a terrible blow.

The Germans were waiting to invade

The Germans got ready for the invasion. About a quarter of a million soldiers were waiting in France. There were about 600 tanks.

There were over 35,000 vehicles. All the Germans had to do was to destroy the R.A.F. They felt that they were nearly there.

The Germans bombed London

Then suddenly and without warning the Germans stopped bombing the airfields. The R.A.F. breathed a sigh of relief. The Germans bombed London. It was probably a mistake. It made the British very angry. The British bombed Germany. The Germans carried on bombing London. This was horrible if you lived in London. But it was a good thing for the Battle of Britain.

The blitz of London had begun. The Battle of Britain was nearly over.

The 15 September was an important day. The battle raged all day. Britain threw in every fighter she had. There were no reserves at all. One pilot wrote in his diary: 'The whole German Air Force seemed to be airborne. Action everywhere and on every sortie. By the end of the day I was tired, annoyed at being shot at so often, and feeling sick, but I couldn't bear to take a day off. It made me feel worse.'

At the end of 15 September the Germans had lost 60 planes and the British had lost 26. For the next few days the weather was bad. Britain held her breath but the worst was over.

Too late for invasion

Hitler realised that he had not destroyed the R.A.F. There was no more time left. If he did not invade Britain in the next week or so it would be too late. He would have to leave it until after the winter. Britain was saved.

The fighter pilots had fought hard day after day. The men who built and looked after their fighters had worked long hours. They had done a good job. The Prime Minister, Winston Churchill, said: 'Never in the field of human conflict was so much owed by so many to so few.' What do you think he meant?

Statistics of the battle (10 July 1940—31 October 1940)

German aircraft destroyed					1,733
R.A.F. fighters destroyed					1,173
Nationalities of pilots who flew with the R.A.F.:					
United Kindom	2,429	Canadian	90	French	13
Australian	21	Rhodesian	2	American	7
New Zealand	102	S. African	21	Czechoslovak	86
Polish	141	Belgian	29	Others	11
R.A.F. fighter pilots and air gunners killed in the battle					510
Luftwaffe airmen killed or captured					approximately 3,368

Things to Do

1 Fill in the gaps. (*Numbers in brackets refer to text line numbers.*)
The Germans wanted to invade Britain. First of all they had to —————————— (2) the British Air Force. The Germans bombed —————————— (7) and —————————— (9). The British were running out of fighters and ——————— (92). Then suddenly the Germans stopped bombing the airfields. They started to bomb ——————— (129). This saved the R.A.F.

2 Why do you think radar stations were difficult to bomb? (Look at the drawing of radar on page 22.)

3 Why do you think British people hoped for bad weather in the Battle of Britain?

4 Do the crossword.

Numbers in brackets after some clues refer to text line numbers.

ACROSS

1 'He said that the —————————— must be bombed so that no planes could use them.' (7)

5 'If the radar stations were knocked ——— how long could the fighters keep going?' (23)

6 Opposite of lose.

7 Short for General Practitioner.

10 'The most famous of the sector airfields were ——————— ————— and Hornchurch.' (109)

12 'The most important ones were the ——————— airfields.' (107)

15 'It was called the —————————— beacon.' (65)

DOWN

1 '——— the bomber had to do was fly along the beam.' (64)

2 'Never in the field of human conflict was so much owed by so many to so ———.' (171)

3 'There seemed to be thousands of Messerschmitts, Spitfires and Hurricanes all mixed up in ——— fights.' (43)

4 'Her —————— was running out.' (100)

8 'I watched pieces of flaming aircraft ———— into the sea.' (53)

9 'In August Hitler gave ——— following order.' (1)

11 'The Germans ——— ready for the invasion.' (118)

12 'British hearts ————.' (22)

13 'I dived ———— on its tail to sea level.' (48)

14 'They had done a good ———.' (167)

10 THE WAR AT SEA

The navies

At the beginning of the war Britain and France together had a bigger and better navy than Germany. The British felt that their navy would keep them safe. However, things changed. France gave up in 1940. That meant that Britain had to rely on her navy alone. Look at the table showing how many ships Britain, France and Germany had in 1939.

Which country had the most battleships? Of which sort of ship did Britain have the most? Which country was building the largest number of submarines?

Then Italy came into the war on Germany's side. Britain had to face the navies of Germany and Italy together.

British ships were old

Many of the British ships were very old. For instance, out of fifteen big ships, thirteen were more than twenty years old. There were not enough destroyers. A destroyer was a fast ship with heavy guns. It had very little armour. There were not enough aircraft carriers.

The jobs of the British navy

The ships in the British navy had a great deal of work to do. These were their main jobs. Firstly, they had to defend Britain. They had to stop the Germans from invading Britain. Secondly, the navy had to look after merchant ships. Merchant ships brought food and other goods to

	BRITAIN		FRANCE		GERMANY	
	Number of ships	Ships being built	Number of ships	Ships being built	Number of ships	Ships being built
Battleships and battle-cruisers	15	5	8	3	2	2
Aircraft carriers	7	6	1	1	—	1
Pocket battleships	—	—	—	—	3	—
Cruisers	64	19	50	3	8	2
Destroyers and torpedo boats	184	38	40	24	22	3
Escorts	46	27	13	8	38	4
Submarines	58	24	71	13	57	40
Motor torpedo boats	27	12	3	6	17	—

The battleship Barham *with more of the fleet in Scapa Flow.*

Britain. Thirdly, the navy had to carry soldiers for the army. Fourthly, the navy had to attack ships taking food to Germany.

Submarines and mines

There were many new inventions that made the navy's jobs hard. There were submarines. Submarines sailed underneath the water. This made them difficult to find. The Germans called their submarines U-boats. The U-boats could attack ships from under the water.

There were magnetic mines. These were undersea bombs. They blew up when a metal ship went near them.

The Germans controlled a great deal of Europe. They could keep their ships right round the coast of Europe. This meant that German ships never had far to go to fill up with fuel and food.

A captured U-boat being examined in a British port.

Parts of Europe occupied by Germany.

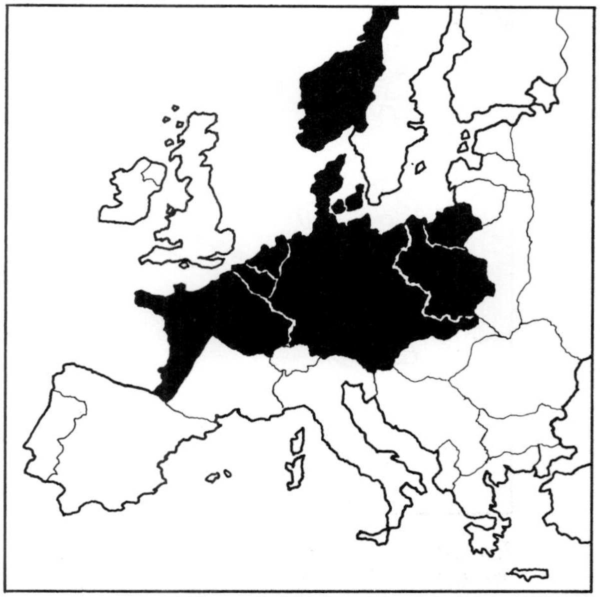

When the war started Britain had ships all over the world. Britain warned them all by radio. They must look out for German ships. The war had started. The Germans would attack all British ships on sight. No British ship was safe.

Britain needed food

There were about 40 million people living in Britain. There was not enough food in Britain for all these people. Britain bought food from other countries. It came to Britain by ship. She bought a great deal of food and other useful things from America and Canada.

Germany wanted to sink all ships bringing food to Britain. Germany would use her U-boats to do this.

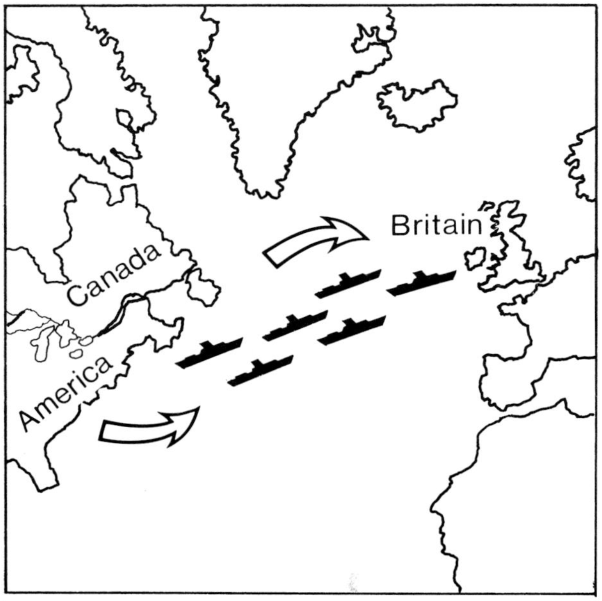

Route of ships going from America to Britain across the Atlantic Ocean.

A convoy escorted by a Sunderland flying boat.

Britain was afraid. Winston Churchill was the British Prime Minister. He said that the U-boats were the only things that really frightened him in the war. If the U-boats sank too many British ships, Britain would starve.

The convoy system

The navy worked hard to look after British ships. They brought in the convoy system. Ships were safer in large numbers. They could be looked after by destroyers and aeroplanes. The destroyers sank the U-boats.

The battle between the British ships and the German U-boats was very important. It went on from 1939 to 1945. It was a desperate battle—a battle for Britain's life. It was called the Battle of the Atlantic. The Atlantic Ocean was where the most important fights took place.

U-boats

Ships could be sunk in four ways. Firstly, they could be sunk by aeroplanes. Secondly, they could be sunk by warships. Thirdly, they could be sunk by U-boats. Fourthly, they could be sunk by mines. Most British ships were sunk by U-boats.

The Germans built many U-boats. The U-boats fought together in groups. They were called 'wolf packs'. Their hunting was deadly. A large 'wolf pack' would attack a convoy of ships. The destroyers tried to sink the U-boats. There were so many U-boats that one or two of them could slip into the convoy and sink the merchant ships easily. In the first half of 1942 U-boats sank 586 ships. This was terribly serious for Britain.

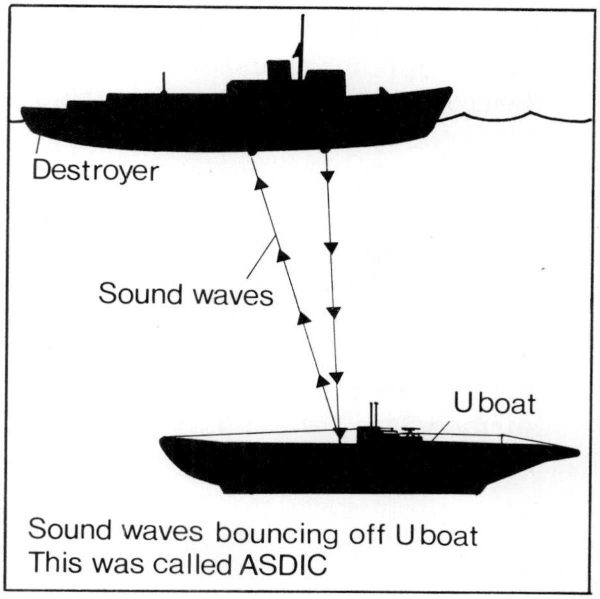

ASDIC

A destroyer throwing depth charges on to a U-boat.

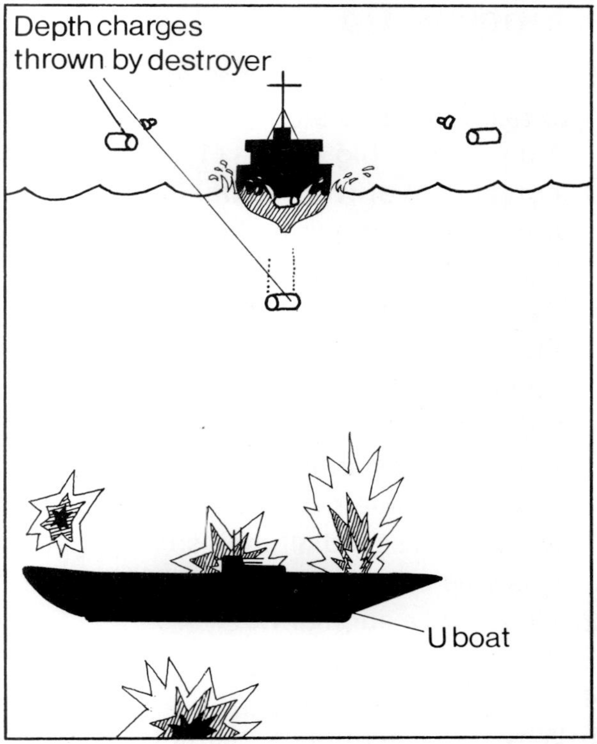

ASDIC and depth charges

The convoy system was not enough. Luckily there were some other answers. One of these was ASDIC. It showed if there was a U-boat under the water. When the destroyer had found the U-boat it could drop its depth charges. A depth charge was a powerful bomb. It was dropped into the sea to blow up a U-boat.

Radar and Schnorkels

Another way to find U-boats was by using radar. U-boats cannot always stay under the water. They have to come up for air. The U-boats came up at night. Radar sets were fitted to British aeroplanes. The radar found the U-boats in the dark. The pilots of the aeroplanes then told the destroyers where to find the U-boats.

Very slowly the U-boats were defeated. By 1944 British convoys were much safer. But they still had to be careful. Germany kept building many U-boats. They made some new inventions too. A schnorkel was invented. This meant that U-boats did not have to come up to the surface. One U-boat stayed under water for fifty days.

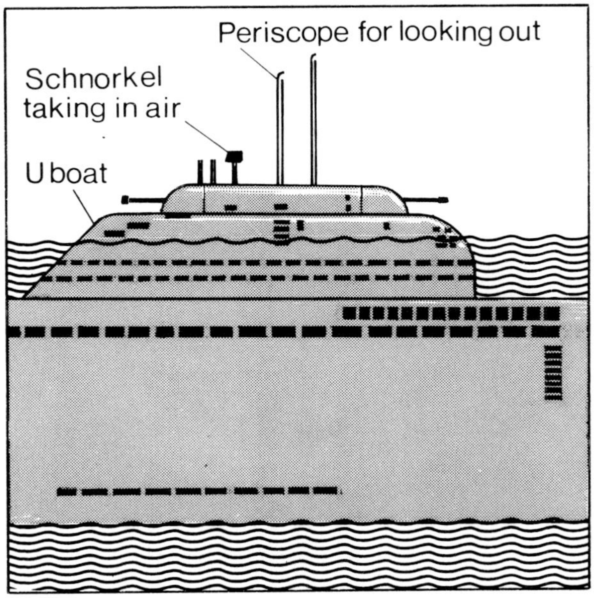

The schnorkel.

Things to Do

1 Fill in the gaps. (*Numbers in brackets refer to text line numbers.*)
Britain had a big ———— (1). But it had a great deal of work to do. One of the jobs was looking after merchant ————— (33). These ships brought food to Britain. If Germany stopped food coming to Britain she would —————— (79). Much food came from Canada and ——————— (69). The Germans used submarines to sink the ships bringing the food. These submarines were called – ————— (44). The British sailed all their ships together. This was called a —————— (83).

2. What was a submarine?

3 What was a 'wolf pack'?

4 What did ASDIC do?

5 Why was a schnorkel useful for U-boats?

11 THE GRAF SPEE AND THE BISMARCK

The Graf Spee *on fire and sinking.*

The *Graf Spee*

There were some very exciting sea battles. One battle was with a German pocket battleship. It was called the *Graf Spee*.

The *Graf Spee* was commanded by Captain Langsdorff. He sailed from Germany on 21 August 1939. He was ordered to stay in the Atlantic Ocean. He was told to sink as many British ships as he could. He sunk nine British ships. He captured some others. The British were desperate to catch him.

All British ships were told to look out for the *Graf Spee*. Altogether twenty-one warships were looking for the *Graf Spee*. That was in December 1939.

The *Ajax*, *Achilles* and *Exeter*

The *Graf Spee* was seen on 13 December. Three British ships attacked her. The ships were the *Ajax*, the *Achilles* and the *Exeter*.

They attacked from different sides. The fight was not easy. The *Graf Spee* had much better guns than the British ships. The *Graf Spee* had guns that could fire at an enemy eighteen miles away. The British guns could only fire at an enemy twelve miles away.

The *Graf Spee* turned her biggest guns on the *Exeter*. The *Exeter*'s guns were knocked out. She kept on chasing the *Graf Spee* but she was soon a battered wreck. She had to leave the fight. The *Achilles* and the *Ajax* stayed on. They would not let the *Graf Spee* get away. They were both damaged but they steamed after the German ship. The *Graf Spee* was damaged too. She threw up smoke screens. She made for the port of Montevideo.

Montevideo

Montevideo was a neutral port. Fighting ships could not stay there for more than twenty-four hours. Captain Langsdorff had his wounded sailors looked after. He had some repairs done. He wanted to make a run home to Germany. The British ships sat outside Montevideo and waited.

The end of the *Graf Spee*

'At 6.15 p.m. watched by immense crowds, the *Graf Spee* left harbour and steamed slowly seawards, awaited hungrily by the British cruisers. At 8.54 p.m. as the sun sank, the *Ajax's* aircraft reported: '*Graf Spee* has blown herself up.'

Captain Langsdorff had been ordered to destroy the *Graf Spee* by Hitler. Langsdorff loved his ship. He was heartbroken. Three days later he shot himself.

The *Bismarck*

Another great hunt took place in 1941. The Germans had built a huge new battleship. It was called the *Bismarck*. It was very fast. The British knew that the *Bismarck* was a very dangerous ship. They made up their minds to destroy the *Bismarck*.

The British sent some of their best ships to hunt the *Bismarck*. One of these ships was called the *Hood*. The *Bismarck* blew up the *Hood*. Then the *Bismarck* went on her way. But more British ships were closing in on her. On 26 May a small aeroplane fired a torpedo at the *Bismarck*. This jammed her rudder. The *Bismarck* lost speed. She also lost control of where she was going. The big British battleships closed in for the kill. They pounded the helpless *Bismarck*. She was soon a blazing wreck. She turned over and sank.

The Bismarck.

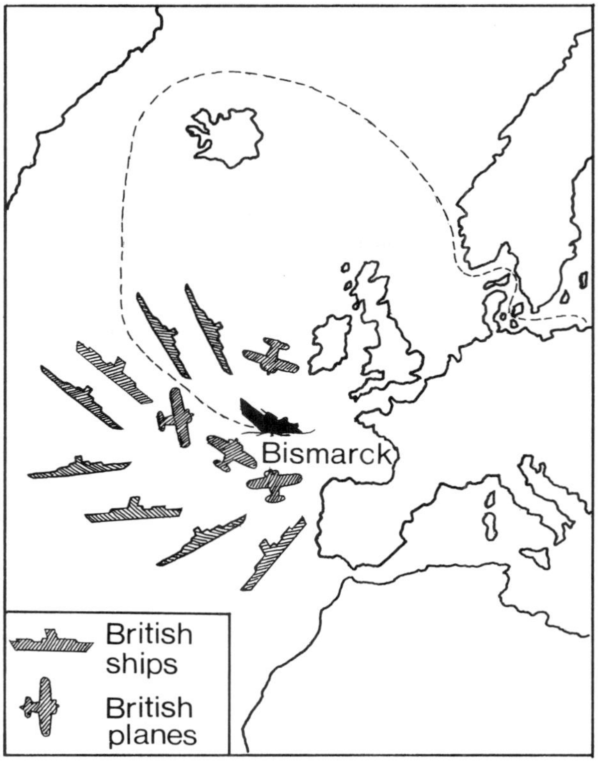

The end of the Bismarck.

The end of the *Bismarck*

Only 110 men were saved. This was out of 2,300 on the *Bismarck*. All the British sailors who blew up the *Bismarck* were sad. She was a wonderful ship. They hated to see her die. But if she had been left alone she would have sunk many British ships.

The end of the *Bismarck* was important in another way. The Germans knew that the British would destroy other large ships too. They decided to use U-boats a great deal more. Firstly, it was more difficult for the British to catch U-boats. Secondly, a U-boat was cheaper to build than a ship like the *Bismarck*.

Sea battles all over the world

The war at sea never stopped. It went on all over the world from 1939 to 1945. There was fighting in the Mediterranean Sea. There was fighting in the Arctic Ocean. This was because the Russians came into the war. They were on the same side as the British. The British tried to help them. They sent tanks and guns to Russia. These tanks and guns went in convoys of ships. They were attacked by the Germans in the Arctic Ocean. The British fought the Italian navy too. The Italians were on the Germans' side.

The Japanese came into the war as well. They were on the side of Germany. The Japanese fought many battles at sea. These battles were against the Americans.

Wherever there were ships there were battles.

For Britain the most important battles were with the German U-boats. These battles were in the Atlantic Ocean. If the German U-boats had won, Britain would have had to give up. She could not have gone on fighting without the food and other supplies coming from America.

Things to Do

1 Fill in the gaps. (*Numbers in brackets refer to text line numbers.*)
The war at – – – (104) never stopped. The Russians came into the war on the same side as the – – – – – – – – (110). The Japanese came into the war on the same side as – – – – – – – (120). Wherever there were ships there were battles. For Britain the most important battles were with the German – – – – – – (126). These battles were in the – – – – – – – – – (128) Ocean.

2 Why do you think the British sailors were sad to see the German *Bismarck* sink?

3 Do the crossword.

Numbers in brackets after some clues refer to text line numbers.

ACROSS

1 'It was called the – – – – – – – – –.' (3)
4 'He wanted to make a – – – home to Germany.' (49)
6 'She kept chasing the *Graf Spee* but she was soon battered – – – – –.' (33)
7 '– – – battle was with a German pocket battleship.' (2)
8 'The Japanese came into the war – – well.' (119)
9 'The British sent some of their best ships to hunt the – – – – – – – – –.' (72)
11 'On 26 May a – – – – – – aeroplane fired a torpedo at the *Bismarck*.' (78)
14 'The British ships – – – outside Montevideo and waited.' (50)
15 Large tool for chopping.
16 'Only one hundred and – – – men were saved.' (87)

DOWN

1 'They were on the side of – – – – – – – –.' (120)
2 Short for prisoner of war.
3 'The *Graf Spee* turned her biggest guns on the – – – – – – –.' (31)
5 Opposite of yes.
9 'The British sent some of their – – – – ships to hunt the *Bismarck*.' (72)
10 'The ships were the – – – –, the *Achilles* and the *Exeter*.' (21)
12 Opposite of woman.
13 'They would not – – – the *Graf Spee* get away.' (37)

12 D-DAY: 6 JUNE 1944

Flags and badges of Britain, America and Russia. ▶

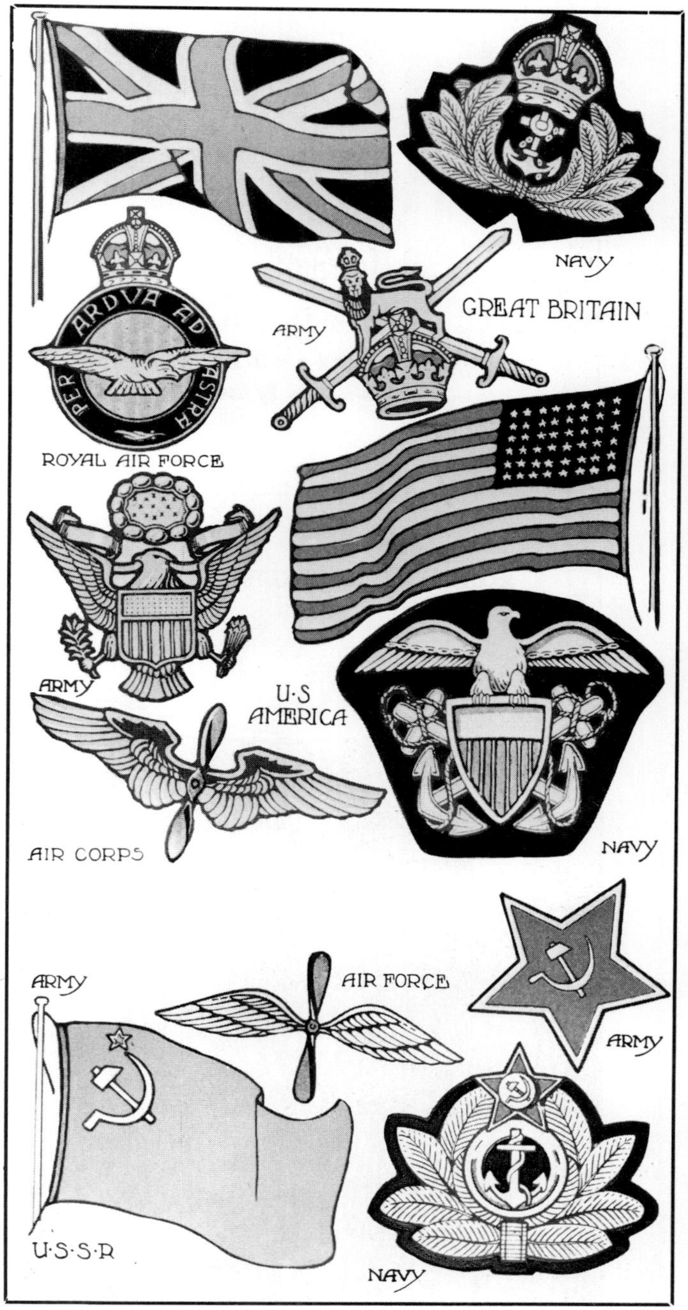

The Allies

The Second World War dragged on. Britain, America and Russia were the chief Allies. They worked and fought to defeat Germany. By 1944 the Allies were strong. They decided to send a large army from Britain. The Allied army would free Europe. It would fight its way to Germany.

D-day

The day chosen for the Allies' invasion was given a code name. It was called D-Day. It was planned for June 1944. June was a good month because the weather should be fine and the tides just right for a landing.

Where to land?

It was difficult to know where to land. All round the coast of Germany and France there were guns, forts, minefields and barbed wire on the beaches and cliffs. The Germans were going to make it difficult for the Allies to land in Europe.

The best route for the Allies to take would have been the shortest one. The Germans knew this too. They had put their largest guns and strongest forts to guard the narrow part of the English Channel. The map shows where the Germans had most of their guns and men. The Allies had to think again.

What were the beaches like?

The Allies had to know what the French beaches were like. This was important because they were going to land thousands of men, tanks and lorries.

The Allies found out about the beaches in a number of ways. Firstly, planes were sent to fly up and down the French coasts. They took photographs from the air. Secondly, French holiday guide books were read. Thirdly, the B.B.C. asked for holiday photos from anyone who had ever been to the French seaside. Ten million photos were sent in! Fourthly, all sorts of sailing books were read to find out about tides and rocks. Fifthly, French spies sent information about German forts, guns and defences on the French beaches.

Wooden shapes called hedgehogs

and tetrahedra were placed in the sea. Look at the two pictures on the front cover. Why do you think the Germans put hedgehogs and tetrahedra in the sea? What other defences are shown on the cover?

The Normandy beaches

Some French beaches were too rocky for ships and men to be landed on. This left only the parts marked on the map. These beaches were known as the Normandy beaches.

The Allies were still worried. The sand might be very soft. Tanks would sink in soft sand. They sent over a brave soldier called Colonel Sam Bassett to find out how soft the sand was. A submarine took him across from Britain to the Normandy beaches. It was a cold, dark, winter's

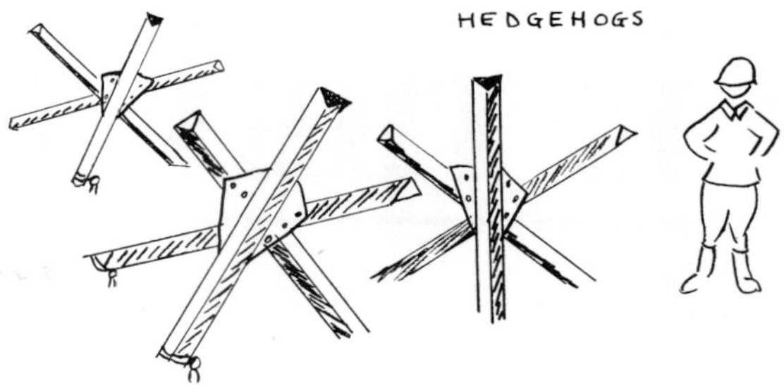

night. He was rowed ashore in a small boat. He had a torch and a small spade. The torch was a special infra-red torch which let him see without being seen by the Germans. He dug over two hundred holes in the sand. All the time he prayed that German soldiers would not shine searchlights on the spot where he was. It was all right. He came back to Britain safely. The sand was hard. Tanks could drive over it, he said.

Things to Do

1 Who were the chief Allies fighting against Germany in 1944?
2 What was the Allied army going to do?
3 What was the code name given to the Allies' invasion?
4 Why was it important for the Allies to know what the French beaches were like?

Colonel Bassett on the enemy beach.

13 THE SHIPS FOR D-DAY

The Allies had many problems to solve. They had to attack the Germans with a large army. Even on the Normandy beaches there were many strong German defences and many soldiers. The Allied army might easily be pushed back into the sea.

The Allies decided to build an enormous fleet of ships. They used about 7,000 ships. About 4,000 of these were ships that would land the soldiers and their weapons.

The other 3,000 ships were either to bombard the Germans from the sea or to carry such things as food, medicine and ammunition. More than three-quarters of the 7,000 ships were British.

This drawing made in 1944 shows ships used in the invasion fleet. The ships include:

1. Troop-Carrying Assault Ships which carried many soldiers.
2. Landing Craft Flak which had many anti-aircraft guns.
3. Landing Craft Infantry which carried 240 soldiers.
4. Landing Ship Tank which carried 60 tanks.
5. Small Landing Ship Tank.
6. Landing Craft Tank which could run right up to the beach.
7. Landing Craft Assault which carried 36 soldiers.
8. D.U.K.W. which was an amphibious lorry.

Work out which is which.

Everything had to be taken to Normandy

All these ships were needed because the Allies had to take everything with them. They took everything from tanks to chewing gum. One officer said that it was like moving the whole of a big city to France.

Large ships cannot sail up to a sandy beach because the water is too shallow. But large ships would be needed to bring over all the lorries, ambulances, tanks and food. About 156,000 soldiers were landed on the first day of the invasion (D-Day). More and more men were landed every day. They were going to fight their way right across to Germany.

Think of a classroom that is 25 feet ($7\frac{1}{2}$ metres) long, 25 feet ($7\frac{1}{2}$ metres) wide and 10 feet (3 metres) high. That is a big class-room. You would need about four big classrooms to hold the food for the soldiers for one day. By September 1944 there were 2 million Allied soldiers on their way to Germany. They all had to be fed.

Harbours or 'mulberries'

Harbours were needed for the large ships bringing things over to Normandy from Britain. The Allies knew that they could not take any harbours from the Germans. The Germans would destroy them rather than let the Allies take them.

The Allies decided to make their own harbours. They were made of

Building part of a Mulberry harbour. Notice the bulldozers clearing away the mud so that the pierheads can be floated out to sea.

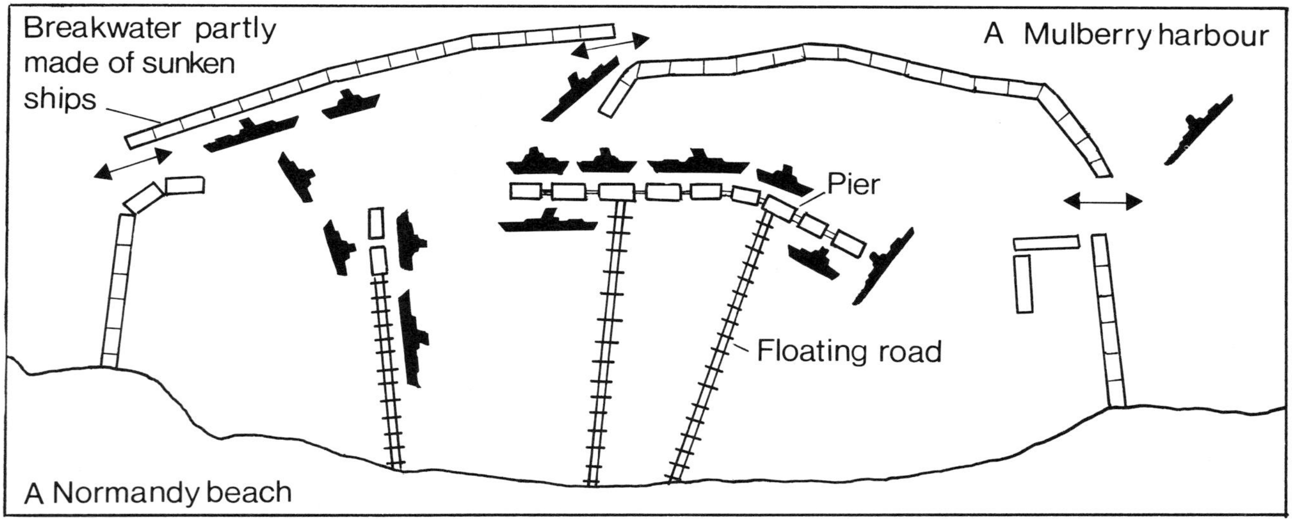

Plan of a Mulberry harbour.

concrete and steel. They were made in Britain. They were then towed across the Channel and anchored by the Normandy beaches. Their code name was Mulberry.

The Allies did not want the Germans to find out what the Mulberries were. Therefore, they made them in separate parts. They could then be fitted together like a jigsaw puzzle. One part would be made in the north of Britain. Another part would be made on the River Thames. No one had ever put all the pieces of the Mulberries together. The first time they were fitted together was in Normandy. A group of 150 strong tugs towed the pieces across to Normandy. They were fitted together to make a harbour and a floating road to the beaches, right under the Germans' eyes.

Many things were unloaded from the ships at the piers. Then lorries brought them along the floating roadway.

View along the floating roadway from the pierhead.

Things to Do

1 How many ships were used for D-Day?
2 Why did the Allies need all these ships?
3 How many soldiers were landed on D-Day?
4 What was a Mulberry made of?
5 How were the Mulberries taken to Normandy?
6 Look at the drawing on page 46. Write a list of all the different sorts of ships.

14 'HOBART'S FUNNIES' AND KEEPING THE D-DAY PLANS SECRET

Major-General Sir Percy Hobart.

'Funnies'

Other clever machines were made. Some of these were called 'Hobart's Funnies'. Major-General Hobart was head of the 79th Armoured Division. He worked out ways of getting through the German defences on the Normandy beaches. There was a bridge-carrying tank, a mine-sweeping tank (called a crab tank), and a swimming tank.

A Churchill tank fitted with a bridge advancing on Le Havre.

A Sherman mine-sweeping tank with the chain flail in action.

A Sherman swimming tank.

Keeping D-Day secret

The Germans knew that the Allies were going to attack them. This was because German aeroplanes had seen the troops, tanks, lorries and ships that were being collected in the south of Britain. Also German spies sent reports back to Germany from Britain.

It was terribly important that the Germans did not know where the Allies were going to attack. If they knew they would be ready and waiting. The Allies pretended that the invasion would be across the narrow part of the English Channel. Many soldiers and tanks were stationed near Dover. Dover was the British port on the narrowest part of the English Channel. Many of the tanks and lorries were made of wood. They were just to fool the Germans. Another thing that the Allies did was to send bombers across the narrow part of the Channel. They bombed bridges, railways and factories.

It was important to keep the D-Day plans secret. Only a handful of top officers knew all the D-Day plans. There were one or two terrible scares.

A windy day in London

One morning the windows were open at the headquarters in London. Twelve copies of the D-Day plans blew into the street. Officers raced out of the building. They were soon seen running up and down among the buses and cars, picking up sheets of paper. Only eleven copies of the plans were picked up. Where was the twelfth? For two hours it was like a nightmare. Suppose the twelfth copy was in the hands of a German spy? The Second World War might be lost. Suddenly an ordinary Englishman knocked at the door. He handed in the twelfth copy of the D-Day plans. He had found it in the gutter. He thought it might be important!

American B17 Flying Fortresses dropping their bombs as they reach the smoke marker over the target.

D-DAY PLAN
Hey! Look out!!!
D-DAY N
I'm sorry we could find only eleven sets of plans!!
One set of plans for the invasion has been lost!!
D-DAY PLAN
Excuse Me. I found these papers....... they were in the gutter. I wondered if they were important?!!

Picking up the last of the dead officers.

Ten D-Day officers died

Another scare lasted longer. A German submarine sank an Allied ship. On the ship were ten officers who knew the D-Day plans.

The Allies were terrified that these men might have been caught by the Germans. Another thing that might have happened was that the bodies might be washed up and found by the Germans. If there were any D-Day plans on them, the secret would be out. The Allies were worried until they found the bodies of all ten officers. They were fished out of the water all stiff in their life jackets. The secret had not reached the Germans.

Things to Do

1 Do the crossword.

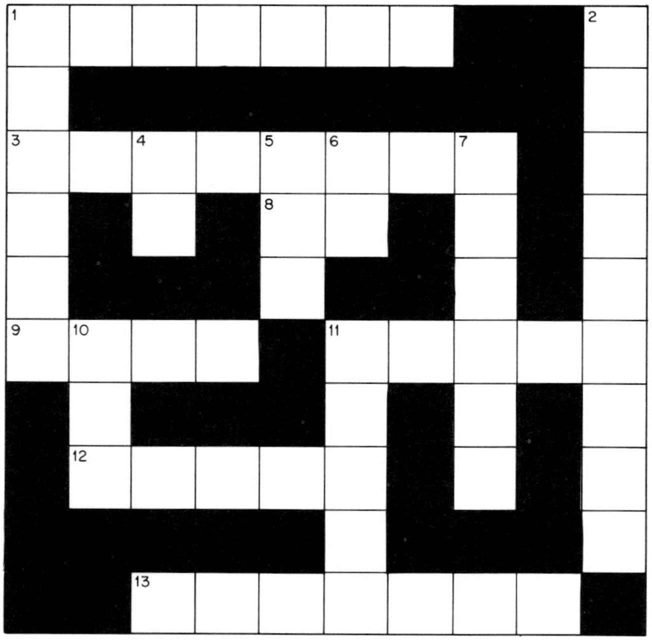

Numbers in brackets after some clues refer to text line numbers.

ACROSS

1 'Only a – – – – – – – – of top officers knew all the D-Day plans.' (37)

3 'Officers raced out of the – – – – – – – – – –.' (44)

8 'Suddenly – – ordinary Englishman knocked at the door.' (54)

9 'A crab – – – –.' (9)

11 'They were fished out of the – – – – – – all stiff in their life jackets.' (72)

12 '– – – – – – was the British port on the narrowest part of the English Channel.' (27)

13 'One morning the – – – – – – – – were open at the headquarters in London.' (41)

DOWN

1 'Major-General – – – – – – – was head of the 79th Armoured Division.' (3)

2 'A German – – – – – – – – – – sank an Allied ship.' (59)

4 '– – was terribly important that the Germans did not know where the Allies were going to attack.' (19)

5 'Twelve copies of the D – – – plans blew into the street.' (43)

6 'He handed – – the twelfth copy of the D-Day plans.' (55)

7 'He had found it in the – – – – – –.' (57)

10 'Many soldiers – – – tanks were stationed near Dover.' (26)

11 'The Second – – – – – War might be lost.' (53)

15 WHAT A SOLDIER TOOK ON D-DAY

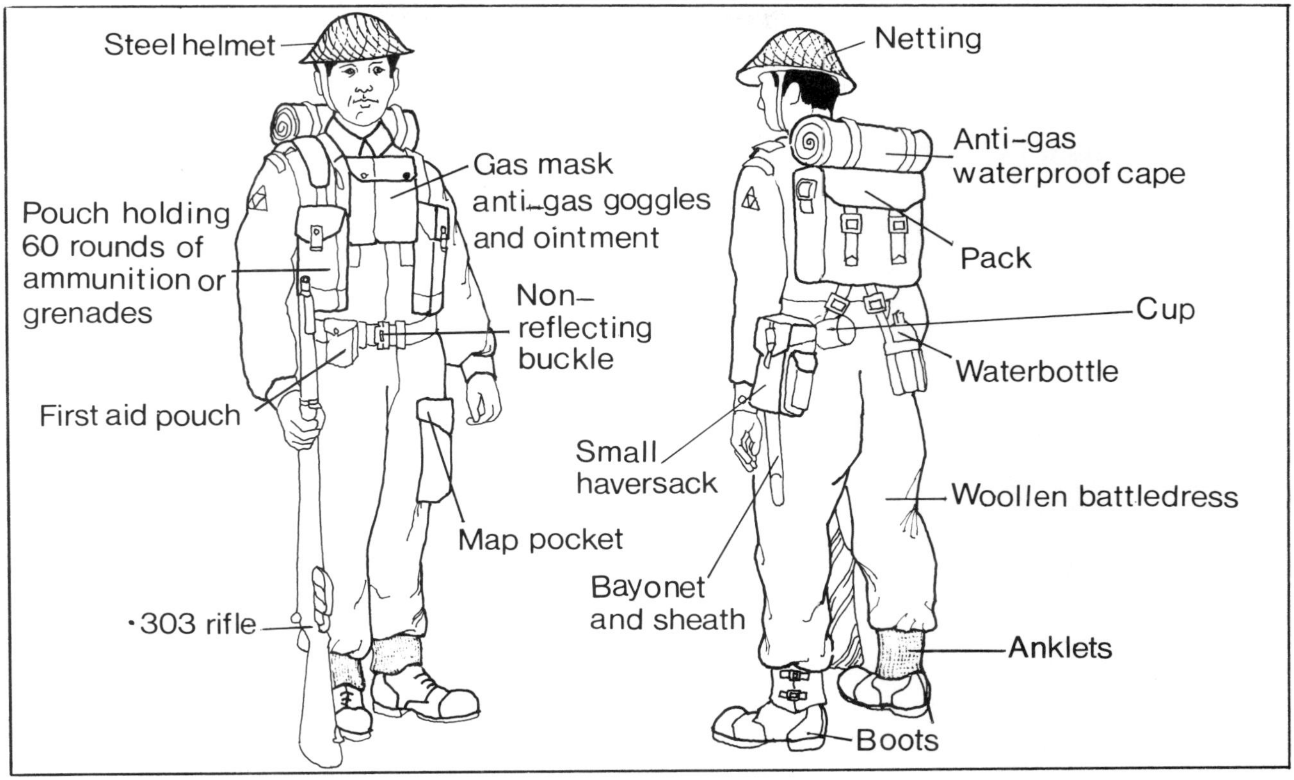

Uniform and equipment of a British soldier.

1. *Why do you think a soldier would have netting on his helmet?*
2. *What does non-reflecting mean? Why would a soldier have non-reflecting buckles?*
3. *What sort of things would the soldier carry in his first-aid pouch?*
4. *What was the bayonet for? How would you use it?*
5. *Why do you think soldiers wore anklets?*

Every soldier had to be clothed, armed and fed. Look at the drawing showing the front and back view of a soldier and answer the questions below it.

Here is a list of all the things a soldier might have with him:

a ground sheet
a greatcoat
pay book
kit bag
spare socks
overalls
waterbottle
canvas shoes
cap comforter
spoon, etc. and mess tin
gloves
underclothes
spare shoes
shaving brush and razor
toothbrush and toothpaste

soap and towel
five brushes
sweater and spare shirt
housewife (needles, etc.)
jack knife
food

All this weighed 55 lbs (that is twenty-five bags of sugar).

On D-Day a soldier would want to take as little as possible with him. Go through the list. What things do you think he would leave out? Remember he has to have enough things to last for twenty-four hours. Why would a soldier want to take as little as possible? Write a list of all the things you would take if you were going away for a day and a night (sleeping in the open).

Food

On D-Day the soldiers would be on their own. Each soldier carried one day's food with him. Here is what a British soldier carried:

ten biscuits
two oatmeal blocks
sugar block
block of tea
milk block
block of meat
one small pack of salt
two gravy tablets
four sugar lumps
one bar of plain chocolate
two bars of raisin chocolate
a few boiled sweets
two packs of chewing gum (this helped sea-sickness)
three pieces of toilet paper
a heater (very small)
fuel blocks

Imagine you are a soldier on D-Day. You are packed in a boat and taken across to Normandy. You wade ashore. You are being shot at. Mines are exploding. You are fighting your way up the beach and into the town until nightfall when you can rest. What would you eat during the day and in the evening? In what order would you eat your food?

16 GETTING READY FOR D-DAY

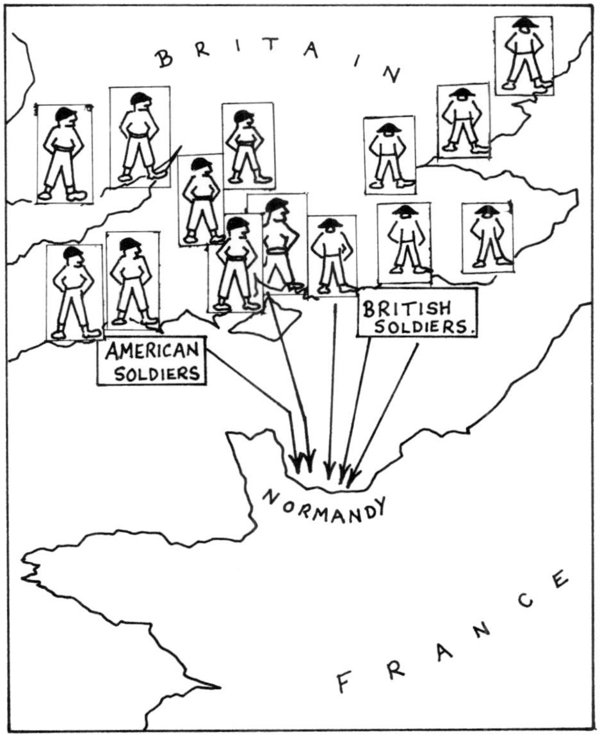

Where British and American forces gathered before D-Day.

Months of training

Soldiers, tanks and lorries were gathered together in the south of Britain. It took several months to train the soldiers. Sailors and airmen had to be trained as well. The navy had to learn how to ferry the army across the Channel. They also had to know how to land the army safely on the Normandy beaches.

Airmen

A large number of airmen were going to be landed in Normandy by parachute. Copies of the German guns in Normandy were built. For months parachute regiments practised capturing them. Other airmen had to learn to fly over the D-Day fleet. Their job was to guard the D-Day ships. They had to see them safely from Britain to Normandy.

Working together

Lastly, the soldiers, sailors and airmen had to learn to work together. Some of the problems were simple but important. There were many different types of Allied aeroplanes. The sailors had to learn to know each type. In the end Allied aircraft were painted with huge black and white stripes. These could be seen clearly from below the plane.

D-Day came nearer. Everyone was excited and scared. The streets of southern Britain were full of lorries and tanks.

Eisenhower

General Eisenhower was put in charge of the D-Day landings. He was American. He was the Supreme Commander over all the Allied soldiers.

He knew that the British might be

Supplies for D-Day pass along a street. How many things in the photograph would you see in a garden and in a street today? How many things are different?

Eisenhower and Montgomery. Find out what part Montgomery played in D-Day. ▶

annoyed at having an American boss. So he worked very hard at being friendly with the British. For instance each American soldier was given a little book about Britain. In the book they were told to be careful what words they used. The word 'bum' in American was all right. In Britain it was rude!

Things to Do

1 Ask at home if any people you know remember D-Day. Show them the photograph opposite. Ask them to tell you what they remember of the troops getting ready to leave on D-Day. Write down what they tell you.

2 Do the crossword.

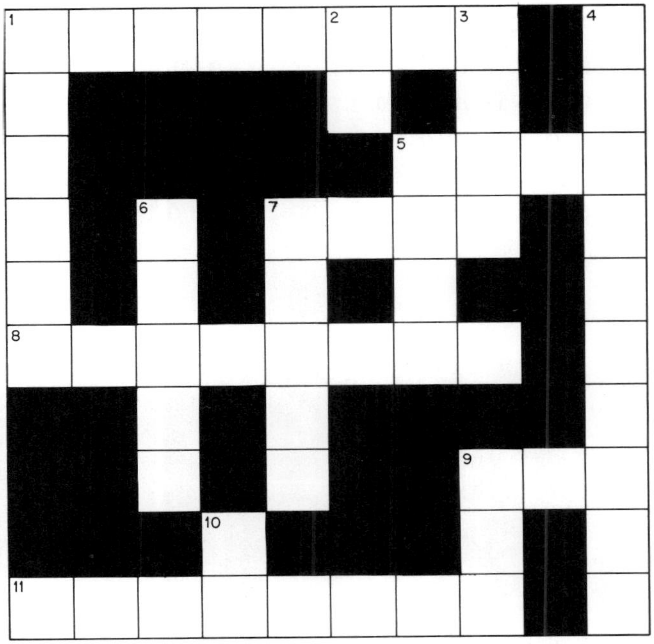

Numbers in brackets after some clues refer to text line numbers.

ACROSS

1 'In the end Allied – – – – – – – – – were painted with huge black and white stripes.' (27)

5 'He knew the British might be annoyed at having an American – – – –.' (40)

7 'For instance each American soldier was given a little – – – – about Britain.' (43)

8 'They also had to know how to land the army safely on the – – – – – – – – – beaches.' (7)

9 Opposite of many.

11 'So he worked very hard at being – – – – – – – – – with the British.' (42)

DOWN

1 'A large number of – – – – – – – were going to be landed in Normandy by parachute.' (10)

2 'Sailors and airmen had to be retrained – – well.' (4)

3 'It – – – – several months to train the soldiers.' (3)

4 'General – – – – – – – – – – – was put in charge of the D-Day landings.' (35)

5 007 was James – – – –.

6 'The navy had to learn how to – – – – – the army across the Channel.' (5)

7 'In the end the Allied aircraft were painted with huge – – – – – and white stripes.' (27)

9 'Other airmen had to learn to – – – over the D-Day fleet.' (15)

10 '– – was the Supreme Commander over all the Allied soldiers.' (37)

17 D-DAY'S HERE!

The fleet set off

Everything was ready by 1 June 1944. The only problem was the weather. There were storms and lashing rain for a week. On 5 June the weather forecast was better. General Eisenhower gave the order for the fleet to sail. Thousands of ships left the harbours of southern Britain. They sailed silently towards Normandy. They were not allowed to speak to each other on their radios. Nor could they speak to the planes overhead.

A rough sea

The sea was rough. The ships rolled and tossed. The men were tense and excited. They had trained for weeks. This was D-Day.

R. N. McKinley of the British Navy remembered:

> I don't think any man that died thought it was him that was going to be killed. The reason we stormed Normandy like we did was because the soldiers would rather have fought the whole German Army than go back on the ships and be as seasick as they were going over.

All the ships sailed together. They had to keep apart. This was difficult. Some ships went faster than others. An American soldier remembered.

> We were on a slow L.C.T. We had a fast British boat behind us. It kept riding up our stern, coming so close we just held our breath. Sometimes we only missed each other by five feet ($1\frac{1}{2}$ metres). We frantically moved to starboard. Then we risked crashing into the boat next to us. This went on all day until we reached Normandy.

Jobs for the airmen

There were three main jobs for the aeroplanes. One job was guarding the ships from German planes. Another job was bombing the German guns in Normandy. A third job was carrying paratroopers. These paratroopers

The invasion fleet on the way.

Paratroopers in an aeroplane, waiting to jump.

1. *What do you think a paratrooper is?*
2. *The men are wearing boots that come higher than their ankles. Why do you think this is?*
3. *Paratroopers often jumped at night. Why?*
4. *Are the paratroopers British or American? How do you know?*
5. *Why do you think some paratroopers darkened their faces with cocoa and oil?*
6. *What other parts of the body would some of them darken?*
7. *What parts of the body are impossible to darken?*
8. *Give two reasons for wearing netting on a helmet.*
9. *What does the white armband with the cross on it tell you about the wearer?*

were dropped in Normandy. They had to destroy German guns near the beaches. They also cut telephone wires. This meant that the Germans could not phone for help.

Paratroopers

About 20,000 men were taken across to Normandy by plane on D-Day. Some landed in gliders. Some wore parachutes and jumped from aircraft.

There was a B.B.C. reporter in one plane: 'We flew over the Channel. A great mass of boats were below us. Then suddenly, there was the noise of flak. There was a deadly silence among us all. I think the plane rocked and jumped. We were praying that our bombers would blow up the German guns soon.'

The paratroopers sat jammed together in the aeroplane. Some had painted their faces with cocoa and oil. They joked that they could lick it off if they got hungry! 'Suddenly a bell rang and a green light flashed. We were over Normandy! We were ready to jump! I crouched by the open door. The air was icy cold but I was sweating. The plane's engines roared. I felt a hard hand in my back. A voice yelled *jump*.'

Many of the paratroopers were lucky. They landed safely. They met together and destroyed German guns. Some men were unlucky. They were machine-gunned down as they landed.

It was early morning on 6 June (D-Day). The paratroopers had landed and done their jobs. The navy arrived with the soldiers.

Things to Do

1 Fill in the gaps. (*Numbers in brackets refer to text line numbers.*)
General ——————————— (5) gave the order for the fleet to sail. The ships sailed silently towards ————————— (9). Some paratroopers had already been dropped. Their jobs were to destroy German ———— (48) near the beaches and to cut ————————— —————— (50).

2 Imagine you are a paratrooper. You are in a plane going to Normandy on D-Day. How do you feel and what do you think about?

3 Do the crossword.

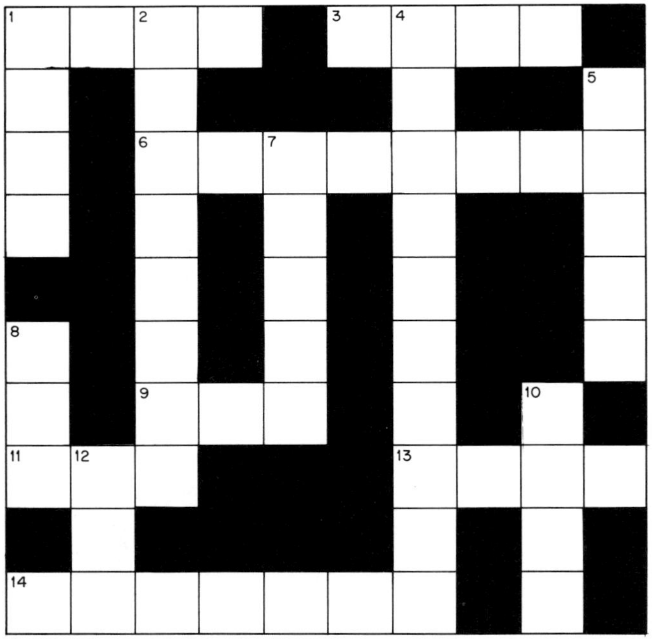

Numbers in brackets after some clues refer to text line numbers.

ACROSS

1 'Everything was ready by 1 ———— 1944.' (1)
3 'I crouched by the ———— door.' (73)
6 'There was a B.B.C. ————————— in one plane.' (57)
9 What you might do if you were very badly wounded.
11 'This was D ———.' (17)
13 Opposite of false.
14 'Some landed in ————————.' (55)

DOWN

1 'There were three main ———— for the aeroplanes.' (42)
2 'They sailed silently towards —————————.' (9)
4 'Some wore ——————————— and jumped from aircraft.' (55)
5 'Suddenly a bell rang and a —————— light flashed.' (70)
7 'About 20,000 men were taken across to Normandy by —————— on D-Day.' (53)
8 'Some ——— painted their faces with cocoa and oil.' (67)
10 'A voice yelled ————.' (77)
12 'There was a deadly silence among us ———.' (61)

18 THE LANDING

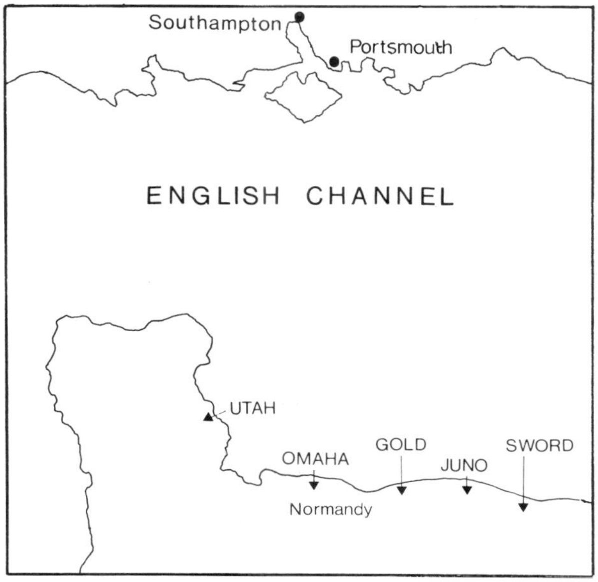

The landing beaches.

The beaches

The Allies landed on five beaches. The beaches had code names. The Americans called their two beaches UTAH and OMAHA. The British called their three beaches GOLD, JUNO and SWORD.

The large ships bombarded the beaches. They wanted to destroy the German guns. If they could do this it would help the soldiers. They were getting ready to jump into the sea and wade ashore.

The sea was terribly rough. The soldiers stumbled ashore. Many of the tanks could not be landed at first. A large number of landing craft sank. Some were hit by mines; some hit the hedgehogs and tetrahedra. Hobart's Funnies were used to clear a path up the beach. Then the soldiers could walk across without being blown up. Even so there was danger. The German guns were firing at the soldiers and ships all the time.

The Germans were surprised, however. They thought the Allies would never land in such bad weather. The main German armies were not in Normandy. The Germans who were in Normandy fought very fiercely.

American troops wading ashore on D-Day. Notice the shell exploding on the shore.

A beach-head on D-Day. Look carefully at the landing craft, trucks, soldiers and barrage balloons.

A roadway laid by US soldiers to help the landing of supplies on a beach.
1. What is the roadway made of?
2. How would it help?

Omaha

The toughest German soldiers were at the beach called Omaha. They were the Wermachts 352nd Division. They fought so hard that the Americans nearly gave up. Many American soldiers were shot to pieces on the sandy beach. There were 3,000 casualties in the first few hours. It was hard for them to know what to do. The Americans had known that this beach would be difficult. They captured it in the end only because they used their finest soldiers. These men were old soldiers of the U.S. 1st Division. At the end of D-Day they had captured 6 miles (10 kilometres) of beach.

It was not so bad on the other beaches. The soldiers waded ashore. Quickly the German guns were destroyed. This made the beaches safe. Then things could be brought ashore.

More and more soldiers poured on to the beaches. Then they moved away. They set off inland. They were on their way to capture Germany.

The mulberries in use

On the day after D-Day, the Mulberries were put together. These huge floating harbours were very useful. Thousands of lorries were landed as well as thousands of men and many thousands of tons of ammunition. The Mulberries meant that all these things could be landed without getting wet.

Slowly the Allies pushed the Germans back. The fighting was hard and bitter. The weeks passed. By the end of June the Allies had far more soldiers in Normandy than the Germans did.

The end of the war

Several German generals knew that Germany should surrender. But Hitler told the Germans to keep fighting. He refused to talk of peace. The Germans fought bravely but the Allies pushed on. The three photographs on the back cover illustrate this.

In August Paris was freed. Then the Allies pushed on again. It took many months to reach Germany. The Germans gave up in May 1945. Hitler shot himself. The Second World War was over.

The drive to Germany.

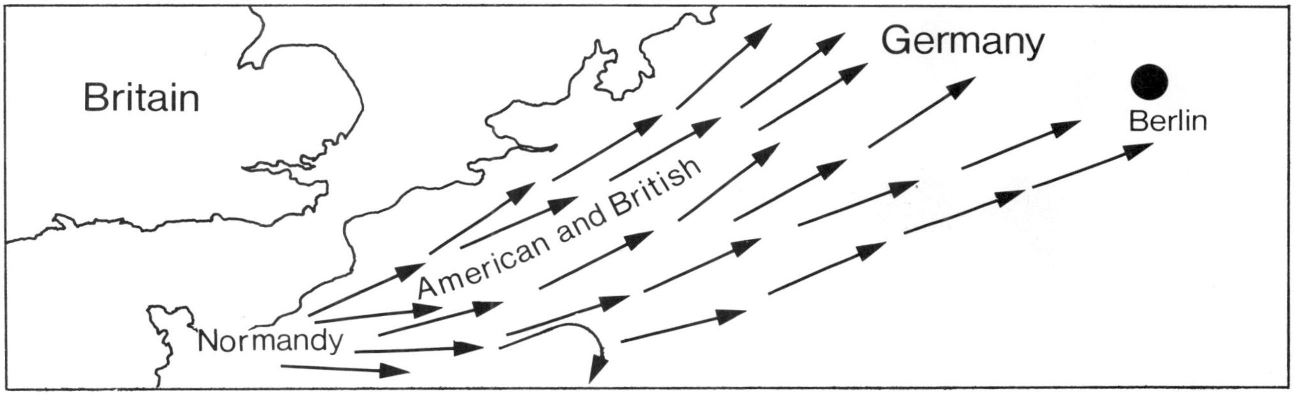

Things to Do

1 Look at the top picture on the back cover. From what country are the soldiers on the left?
2 Look at the middle picture on the back cover. Can you see whether the planes are German or Allied?
3 Make a list of all the weapons you can see on the back cover.
4 Look at the pictures on the back cover. Draw your own picture of the D-Day fighting. You could perhaps trace some pictures from this book to help you.
5 When did the Germans give up?
6 Work out how long it had taken the Allies to win the war from D-Day until the Germans gave up.
7 Do the crossword.

Numbers in brackets after some clues refer to text line numbers.

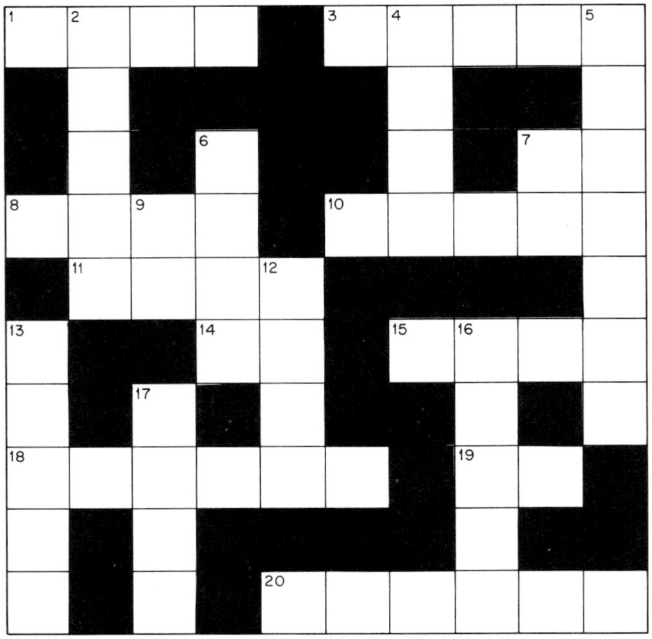

ACROSS
1 The name of the British beach that sounds very rich.
3 'The British called their three beaches Gold, Juno and – – – – –.' (4)
7 It – – many years since D-Day.
8 'Many American soldiers were – – – – to pieces on the sandy beach.' (36)
10 'A large number of landing – – – – – sank.' (16)
11 'They they moved – – – –.' (56)
14 '– – refused to talk of peace.' (77)
15 The second British beach.
18 'They fought so hard that the Americans – – – – – – gave up.' (35)
19 'It was hard for them to know what to – –.' (39)
20 'More and more soldiers – – – – – – on to the beaches.' (55)

DOWN
2 'The toughest German soldiers were at the beach called – – – – –.' (32)
4 Soldiers – – – – battledresses, helmets and boots.
5 'They wanted to – – – – – – – – the German guns.' (8)
6 'The Americans called their two beaches – – – – and Omaha.' (4)
7 '– – they could do this it would help the soldiers.' (9)
9 What you might shout out if you were in pain.
12 To shout out very loudly.
13 'Some were hit by – – – – –.' (17)
16 Opposite of on top.
17 'They were getting ready to jump into the sea and – – – – ashore.' (10)

CONCLUSION:
WHY IT WAS CALLED A WORLD WAR

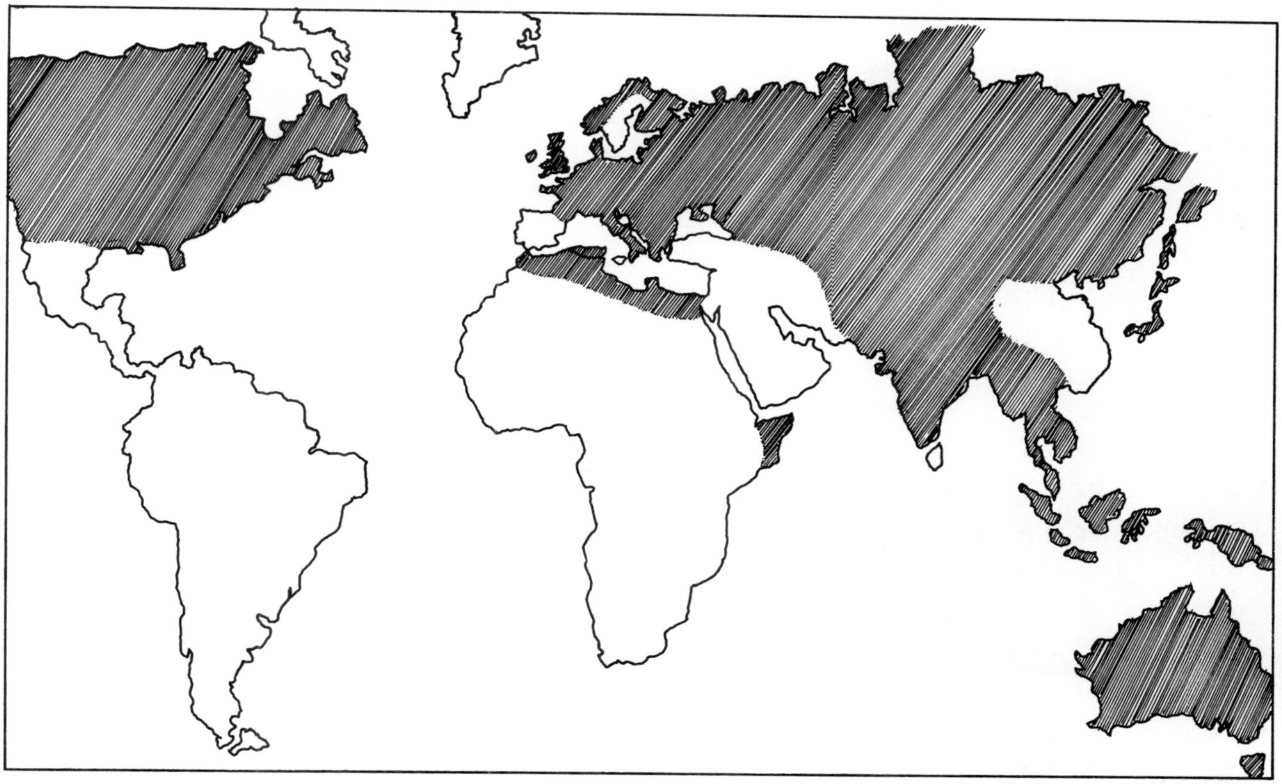

Areas of the world affected by the Second World War.

Fighting went on all over the world. Many countries were brought into the war.

For one thing Britain had an empire. This meant that Britain ruled many other countries. These countries were in different parts of the world. Men from these countries helped Britain to fight Germany. There were soldiers from Canada, Australia, New Zealand, South Africa and other parts of the British Empire.

Also, parts of the British Empire were attacked. This is why the British fought the Japanese. The Japanese took Hong Kong, Malaya and Burma from the British. They also took other land. Japan is a small country. She wanted more land. That is why Japan came into the war.

The Americans came into the war as well. The Japanese attacked them. The Americans also helped Britain to fight the Germans.

Italy joined in the war too. She was on Germany's side. This led to fighting in North Africa, in East Africa and Greece.

Russia joined in the war. She changed sides. She started on Germany's side. Then Germany turned on her. Russia went over to Britain's side. This meant that there was a great deal of fighting in Russia. Germany tried to take Russia. The fighting between Germany and Russia was on a huge scale. The suffering was terrible. Twelve million Russians died. In the end the Russians drove the Germans out of Russia.

American soldiers on the way to Germany in the winter of 1944–5.

Things to Do

1 Find out more about Hitler. Make a scrapbook about him. Why do so many people think he was evil?
2 Find out in detail about the German advance to Dunkirk in 1940. Make a huge wall map for the class-room plotting each day's movements.
3 Visit the Imperial War Museum ('phone 01 735 8922).
4 See if you can find anyone who was in the forces and ask them for details of their life. It would be excellent if you could find someone involved in D-Day. Perhaps you could borrow a cassette or tape recorder and record what they say.
5 Go and see the Overlord Embroidery. It tells the story of D-Day, just as the Bayeux Tapestry tells the story of the Battle of Hastings in 1066. The Overlord Embroidery is at Whitbread's Brewery, Chiswell Street, London, EC1 ('phone 01 606 4455).
6 See if you can find a local war memorial. See how many men from your area died in the Second World War. Can you spot any names of people you know locally? Is there a statue of a soldier? Look at it carefully. Look closely at what he is wearing and carrying.
7 Make a model of one of the D-Day beaches—a large undertaking. Use a really detailed book, e.g. *D-Day* by Warren Tute (published by Sidgwick and Jackson). Include models of tetrahedra and hedgehogs.